I0203691

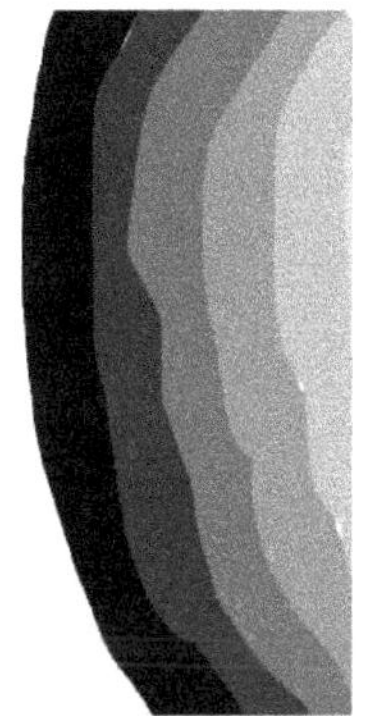

Living Inside the Rainbow

Winning the Battlefield of the Mind After Human Trafficking and Mental Bondage

Brook
Parker-Bello

Living Inside the Rainbow

Winning the Battlefield of the Mind After Human Trafficking and Mental Bondage

Brook Bello: info@moretoolife.org
https://www.brookbello.com
Twitter: @brookbello
Facebook: https://www.facebook.com/LivingInside.TheRainbow
Company: Twitter: @realmoretoolife

ISBN: 978-0-9654415-2-0
Library of Congress Control Number: 2014955880

Editor: Diana Rowan
Cover Design: Otis Spears
Front Cover Photography: Edward Linsmier
Interior Design: John Sibley, Rock Solid Productions

Publisher:
Dr. Brook Parker-Bello
1661 Ringling Blvd., Unit 2212
Sarasota, Florida 34230

Printed in the United States of America

Dedication

To God, My Redeemer,
who has given me hope
and a future so that through
the knowledge of
Your love others may live

"I freed a thousand slaves and could have freed a thousand more, if they only knew they were slaves."

Harriett Tubman

CONTENTS

PART 3
SALVATION IS FREEDOM OFTEN EXPERIENCED IN THE PRESENCE OF UNREST

FOREWORD

With each turn of the pages of Brook Bello's book, I could feel my heart opening wider and wider. Brook's story is a demonstration of God's faithfulness. He said, *"Suffer the little children to come unto me, for such is the Kingdom of heaven…"*.

Brook's story, as she explained it to me, is the victory story of a "woman-child," meaning the horrifically abused child that lived inside a woman's body for so long. This story is full of hope and inspiration: hope for the future of survivors everywhere and inspiration to the families, supporters, advocates and way-makers working on their behalf day in and day out.

I am honored to know Brook, to stand with her as mentor and friend.

You are "the wind beneath the wings" of so many who see their faces in yours. Your story is their story. You have allowed us to see what a survivor looks like through you.

Brook's brilliantly written account of her life can be used as a textbook to teach those working to eradicate human trafficking. This book is a case study on the emotional and psychological state of a victim and the world she had to navigate to survive.

Brook wrote her book, but not to have you feel sorry for her. She does not want or need sympathy. She wants and needs your advocacy in the fight to change the world's view on girls living as she did: in forced prostitution.

My request of you as you read Brook's story is that you not allow yourself to get stuck in the horror of the story. Don't let it overwhelm you. Instead, allow it to move you to action.

What if every person who reads this book commits to one simple action, something that you can do right where you are? It could be something simple, such as supporting an organization that's working to help build awareness in your city or donating money toward resources for survivors. This simple action would make an enormously positive difference in the lives of so many.

Thank you, Brook Bello, for your courage in sharing your story and for your willingness to "Live: *Above the Noise and Inside the Rainbow.*"

BARBARA A. PERKINS
Author, Personal Coach
President, Vanzant Enterprise
President, International Black Women's
Public Policy Institute

ACKNOWLEDGMENTS

I would like to offer a special thank you to Dr. Carroll A. Baltimore, first for co-writing one of the chapters, and for being an amazing spiritual father as I continue on this journey.

Of course, the book grew through me from the start of my journey to wholeness and to founding the More Too Life program and center. I would like to express my gratitude to the many people who saw me through so much in writing this book and creating More Too Life. Thanks to all those who provided support, talked things over, read, offered comments, allowed me to quote their remarks, and assisted in the editing, proofreading, and design.

Thank you, my Ted, for standing by my side as I wrote.

I would like to honor David Arkless and Sarah Summers of Arkless Consulting in Europe for believing in me with funding from the very beginning for More Too Life, Inc.

Special thank you to Dr. Barbara Williams-Skinner for loving me like family, showing me what leadership means, reaching back to help lead the way, and asking me over and over, "Is the book done?" I would like to thank my pastor, Dr. Beverly "Bam" Crawford, for teaching me the ways of God.

I would also like to thank my dear friend and sister, Donna L. Kinsler, for being a great listening ear.

Shanna Biedron, thank you, my sister, for allowing God to use you as you brilliantly encouraged me along the way.

Thanks to Cecelia Garbutt (deceased), who loved me through it all.

Thank you, Diana Rowan, for editing, caring that I wrote the book, and spreading the word. Thank you for empowering, educating, and assisting women and children around the globe.

Further, I would like to thank my friends at Wheelock College in Boston and Jackie Jenkins-Scott for allowing me teach through the sharing of my story.

Attorney Sharon Bridges and the International AKA Sorority, thank you for listening.

Thank you to the White House for allowing me to be a plenary speaker at the 2013 White House Summit to Eradicate Modern Day Slavery, and to President Obama for making this part of your struggle as well.

In addition, thank you to all those who are assisting in the fight to end Modern Day Slavery.

I would also like to thank all of my friends and all family members just for being who you are and moving forward even when it's been hard.

Thank you to each and every victim and survivor of every form of human trafficking and sexual abuse—for your continuous struggle to be free and to fight for the freedom of others. We are listening and we are fighting.

SPECIAL NOTE FROM THE AUTHOR

I was a victim then I became a survivor of child sex slavery. But we who have survived this horror need to move further than that; we need to soar beyond it! With God's help and the support of many, I evolved into being a *thriver*—and now I am simply a "champion." I am a champion as anyone can be who struggles through a grueling battle to victory. And my victory is to tell my story and carry out my work in the world to help others on the path out of sex-slavery and other root causes that can lead from mental bondages caused by violent abuse into healing and wholeness.

Thank you for taking this journey with me, this testimony of God's undying faithfulness. My story is woven throughout the pages, and I tell much of it. My prayer is that it increases your hope for a better future, your faith, awareness, and love like never before. I hope that men and fathers begin to understand that their lack of leadership in the home and with their children throws off a divine rhythm. That even in the best of times a woman with a man of honor at her side does not have to sweat and toil to try and be both father and mother in broken homes. Men are the biggest part of the problem to sexual crimes and violence, rape, commercial sexual exploitation, human trafficking and fatherlessness and so they will be the biggest part of the solution.

Brook Parker-Bello

WHAT OTHERS ARE SAYING

"*Living Inside the Rainbow* is about God's promise of restoration. This process of recovery involves the soul and enlightening of the mind. In this book, Brook's honest and transparent story of spiritual power helps us to consider the contribution of our thoughts to the ultimate result of one's life. 'It is a must-read!'"

Dr. Beverly "Bam" Crawford
Founder and Pastor,
Bible Enrichment Fellowship International Church

I thank God for the power, strength, and courage of the life force that is Brook Bello. We are on the planet to use our gifts—our pain and suffering—to being wholly transparent. We literally breathe life into others when we share our stories with one another. It is the essence of healing—and the only way we can know we are not alone. Thank you, Brook, for standing and living in God's grace. *Living Inside the Rainbow* reminds me of words by Edmund Burke:...'All that is required for the triumph of evil is that good men remain silent and do nothing.' Your book is a clarion call for us to use our voices to put an end to human trafficking."

Terrie M. Williams, Author
Black Pain: It Just Looks Like We're Not Hurting

"Brook, I am sure that this book this will be powerfully freeing and enlightening as you share your traumatic testimony and dramatic deliverance in and through Jesus Christ and other good people who have been Jesus to you along the way."

Pastor David Anderson
Author, Radio Host, and Church Leader

"Human trafficking is the absolute lowest form of inhuman treatment that can be perpetrated by a person or group against another in a free society. The freedom to realize one's God-given potential is crushed almost beyond repair for those trapped as sex slaves—many, like Brook Bello, as children. But Brook Bello simply refused to remain locked in the prison others intended for her and by God's grace and power, broke free, not just physically, but emotionally, psychologically, and spiritually. While still on the road to full restoration, she has committed her life to freeing and nurturing to wellness others trapped in this most evil industry. ***Living Inside the Rainbow*** is a must-read for those who hate evil and want to learn how to help eradicate the human trafficking industry.

Dr. Barbara Williams-Skinner
President, Skinner Leadership

"From rape to redemption, from human trafficking to a transformed life, Brook shares her amazing journey from fear to freedom. I recommend this book to those who are looking for healing, restoration, and their own pathway to freedom."

Rosemary Trible, Author,
President, Fear2Freedom,
Wife of former Senator Paul Trible

"***Living Inside the Rainbow*** by Brook Bello is a must-read book. She reveals her own life's journey of God's Amazing Faithfulness and Grace. Life is not a game, life is a gift...a gift of grace. *Living Inside the Rainbow*, Brook moves from trauma to wholeness. Literally, from "'Grace to Grace'."

Dr. Carroll A. Baltimore, Sr.
President, Progressive National Baptist Convention, Inc.

Part 1

The Importance of Understanding

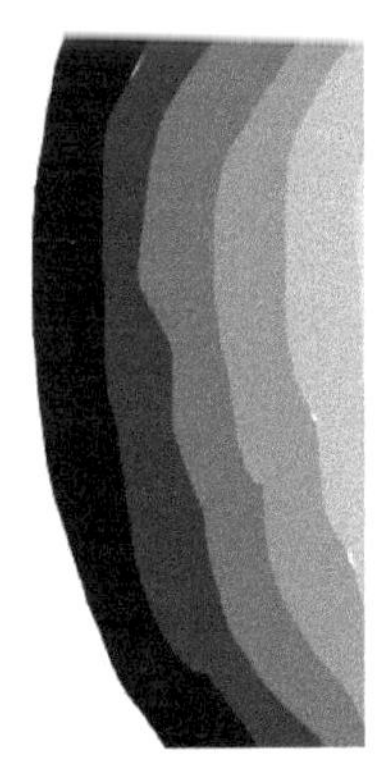

INTRODUCTION

I want to take you on a journey from death to life, from living with and without knowing love, without the Holy Spirit, without the full knowledge of God's true love and what it's like on both sides.
I was shackled to a couple from Middle America, those that I also call traffickers and pedophiles. They are traffickers because supplying human bodies is the biggest part of child sex slavery and human trafficking. They are pedophiles because they rape minors and broken women in the process. They tried to appear safe before me, in a world of evil, but they are evil, with the intention only of selling young bodies for profit. They create in their own minds the sociopathological illusion that the victim wants to be there, that I wanted to be there.

I was picked up from near my school the first time, where I was wandering lonely. I was 15 and lured by the promise of work and friendship. This lead to a process of what I now know is called "grooming." By the time I ran away, months after that, I was broken, a runaway, and with the promise of food and shelter I ended up in a house across town. I did not tell my mother, I was too ashamed and thought it was my entire fault. Unfortunately, this made it easier to eventually run away out of state, where I was picked up by a pimp and his bottom girl. Then, one of the tricks that purchased girls, was also another unassuming couple.

This first time, I was taken to a back room that appeared to be normal but it was a setup; then they pulled out the equipment (sex toys, gadgets, and pornography) that they used on lost children of any gender, especially females. They began to beat one another to show us how it needed to be done. They beat each other horribly in the process of what they called sex, and I assumed at this point that most people were, in fact, like this. Before they hurt me, they raped my mind, our minds. I was already medicated and had sat through a tortured dinner earlier which was meant to facilitate some crazy pretend game that seemed to confuse us kids regarding who they really were and why we were there. I mentioned to someone how I longed for a father and how, after I was raped as a young girl, I so longed to be loved and feel safe enough to tell someone what happened, and that I lost my virginity through rape when I was close to 12 years old. But most rape victims don't tell, and I was no different. It seemed those that groomed us were looking for us, for broken and violated kids because they knew exactly what to say to get into our heads. It reminds me of much of what I now teach about Human Trafficking, victim and predator identification. It's not surprising that 65% of African American females are sexually violated in some form, rape is one of them.

I was trained, through emotional beating and rape—for which they use the perverted term "seasoning," to do what I was told, to pretend that I liked it.

Let me pose a question: What child or even healthy woman would choose brutal and evil intercourse and rape? How can a young mind even gauge it? This is what happens to so many children—young girls and women ranging from the ages of one (yes, one year old) to 18 years of age and up—who often think a protector or friend is just that, a parent or parent figure, true friend, or hero but who turns out to be a pathological predator.

I know of a woman who was taken from her country by missionaries at age two and was raped from that point until she was 18 and after. She was so emotionally damaged that she even called it sex, and would go on later to be prostituted. She would tell the authorities that she was "having sex" at *seven years old.* After being molested, raped, and trafficked from the age of three years old, she still thought it was her fault.

She even thought she desired it, as it was the only form of intimacy she had ever known. Yet her vaginal walls and anal cavity are torn from the years of abuse; she is physically and emotionally scarred. As the sparkle of a match is to a three year old, so is a pimp's fake smile and false love—a shine or glow that a small child/broken teenager thinks is a glimmer of hope. But it is merely a lit match that becomes an enormous fire that burns up everything in its path. The smile of a pimp is one of the worst aspects of trafficking. Hopes, dreams, minds, and lives are burned up in this fire of immoral abuse and the film "Hustle & Flow" states this well as society made this a blockbuster as we watched it and breathed in the abuse of women, as commonplace. The devastating pain and destruction is wrapped in sterile terms like *human trafficking, forced prostitution*, *abuse*, *incest, molestation,* and *child sex slavery/ sex slavery.*

I am praying for two 13-year-old girls that I know of. When they heard my story they could not believe that I had survived and am not only functioning, but also thriving. They were raped from the ages of five to nine by an adult male relative, with other young cousins also in the room. They were ravaged and hung from the ceiling. He cut them and stitched them back up, and their young virginal wounds were raped, pillaged of innocence and sacredness by this elderly male. He sodomized them and raped them for hours. All the while, no one really knew what was going on. I was told the cuts and stitches were explained as issues they were having while playing too roughly outside on the jungle gym. These girls simply cannot believe that I am still here. But because they are still so very young, they have an innocent hope—something that is more natural in younger children but just as possible for all, as we are all God's children.

The fact that their brains are not fully developed is good and maybe not so good. This depends on the assistance they receive, hopefully as soon as possible. If they do receive help, they do have an opportunity to heal more quickly with less discrimination and a little more mercy from others. They will do better than children who have slipped through the cracks and are long forgotten; these innocent young ones still need the same assistance as adults in order to heal and discover, even for the first time, who they really are. They are, with God's love, willing to absorb the possibilities of change. No matter how old you are, I have to share, again, that this really is possible. I am an example of that: God's unrelenting Grace, healing presence, mercy, and supernatural counsel of the Holy Spirit through the Bread of Life found in the Word of God.

What has so blinded the hearts of those who think, even for a moment, that a child desires these violent sexual crimes: to be burned and scarred by the evil of pedophilia? It has become a forest fire that no one seems to understand how to put out. Was there ever such a thing actually or truly experienced as *teenage prostitution*? Or was it just a phrase made up by the ignorant and closed-minded in life who refuse to take a closer look? Are we trying to wrap our heads around the fact that eight-year-old girls are given in marriage around the world? Do men compare in their hearts what they think of as 13- to 16-year-old girls who married in the Scriptures? We don't know *exactly* how old all of the girls in Scripture were. Do some men today evilly believe that incestuous rape, happening today with fathers against daughters, is to be compared with biblical persons marrying half-brothers and the like in a different world and in a different time? Whatever happened in biblical times is over and could never be compared to the pedophilia of today! Even today, people and our world are not the same as they were 70 years ago. Therefore, children need different lifestyle and family structures for healthy psychological development.

The supernatural manifestations of the populating of the earth and what took place in that time is not to be compared with this. This evil, this human trafficking of which forced prostitution is a part, this modern-day slavery, is an abomination. This abomination is being revealed in all its stark horror now, so that we wake up to all forms of bondage and live for God. For in truth, there is nothing else but His love. He is the answer; in God's wisdom and love are all of the answers.

This issue of human trafficking is not one in which mere treatment of the symptoms is going to produce a cure. We need to go deep, to examine the root causes, which are found in discrimination of all kinds and negative and destructive societal pop culture. From focusing too much on self, to gender issues, to ethnic discrimination, economic discrimination, classism, unresolved child abuse, too much unrelenting media violence, evil, and lust without conscience or respect for innocence anymore—it seems that many of these discriminations are at an all-time high. Men's desire *for conquering and to conquer* has put the innocence of children and others in harm's way.

There are also times in church when those in pain do need much more than a song and a sermon to heal. They need to "see" and experience real love in a dying world. Sometimes we give up when healing does not come quickly enough for us. Some people have not seemed to wake up after all of the help they receive. And yet, how can we judge the depth of the hurt that they need to heal from? Healing comes as the Spirit wills, and oftentimes the Lord requires us to be a part of our own healing and the healing of others, on a line-by-line and precept-upon-precept basis. If God said that He would not allow anyone to "suffer above that which they are able to bear," then what we suffer as individuals must be as much as we could possibly ever survive, even if it seems simple to someone else. You see, we can transform after the process, if, in fact, we live beyond it. Our minds can be rewired to a whole wonder of destiny and life, when we make it through.

Let's talk about sex. It is and should be a sacred thing that has to do with knowing one another and is still thought of for many as a part of blissful matrimony. Yet a child or woman with an underdeveloped heart and mind is still a gentle flower, an innocent that must be protected. How do they heal and rebuild from severe abuse? I don't much like using the phrase *sex slavery*. Do you know why? Because, as I will share with you in the book, it relates to a word that means intimacy, and this isn't intimacy.

This is a vile and horrid thing, this human trafficking. I call it "soul assassination."

We are a spirit; we live in a body, and we have a soul, a soul that comprises our will, our mind, and our emotions. Our ability to maneuver in and around who we are in our soul is what is robbed and assassinated. When people hear the word *sex*, something happens in the brain: a heart-body connection that can cause confusion in the outcome of how we see a thing, how we see abuse, how we view the real trauma that takes place when sex becomes a crime, is unwanted, and, moreover, when a child is involved.

There is simply no way a very young child can wrap his or her mind and heart around the abuse they've suffered or, worse, are still going through; it causes severe mental confusion and damage. These days, there is so much severe dysfunction in families and parenting that people often grin about it because it has gotten to be so "normal." Because of the failure to truly have "restorative justice"[1] of one's soul after dysfunction, there is often an underdeveloped child in many adults, one that is just wondering how to grow up, how to "come of age" on every level.

When some teens are 16, they can be ten years of age in certain areas of the heart and mind, which is why I called myself a "woman-child" as I looked back.

I've witnessed the small 11-year-old boy surface to the reality of his 45-year-old chronological self simply when his father faced him head on and said, "Son, I love you, I always have, and I'm so very proud of you." I saw him, the brawn and stature of this six-foot, three-inch, 250-pound man, break down like a small child, an innocent.

What about when there are more of what I have termed "points of impact"? I want you to understand my story in the hopes of bringing greater understanding to these issues: one is that discrimination is a key factor in why minor-aged victims who accuse pedophiles don't get the assistance they need. And often, because of our own dysfunction and brokenness, we have a distorted point of view of the real issues at hand.

This point of view sometimes keeps us from the 1 Corinthians 13 love and mercy that are needed in these times.

Was it only me who felt psychologically disjointed by dysfunction and violence? Or Vednita Carter in Minnesota, or maybe Marlene Carson in Ohio, Rachel Lloyd in New York City, amazing survivor champion Tina Frundt in D.C., Lisa Williams in Georgia, Kristy Childs in Kansas, or other child sex slavery victims and champions? What about the six-month-old baby girl who was raped and bled to death—yes, I said six months old,[2] or the four-year-old girl in India[3] whose womb was ripped to shreds? What is a *child*, birth to ten years of age, or ten to 17 years of age? Can you really determine age-appropriateness for a raped and mutilated womb, which can cause women to have angry wombs later in life with trauma that leads to various vaginal and womb ailments. The physical challenges that I have faced because of what I call "womb trauma" have greatly affected the entire scope of my life.

How about a five-year-old girl that was raped and survived but has never told her story? She is now 22 years of age with her life falling apart around her and doesn't know where to turn. She's addicted to so called sex, does not understand the treasure of being a woman and hasn't experienced justice, comfort, mercy, or truth in society relating to sharing the rape and abuse she suffered. She has no "safe place to fall."

Adults who are 40 years of age who grew up in dysfunction, unable to share their story or get help with the abuse they've suffered, stopped growing in some areas psychologically. Too often they don't realize it until later in life; sometimes, it's too late.

"An Ohio man convicted of imprisoning three women in his house and raping them repeatedly for a decade blamed his actions on a *sex addiction* and said he was 'not a monster' as he was sentenced to life without parole plus 1,000 years. The women disappeared separately between 2002 and 2004, when they were 14, 16 and 20 years old."[4] This, of course, was a major news story in

August 2013 and has set an amazing precedent for successfully prosecuting crimes of pedophilia, kidnapping, and rape/multiple rape. These crimes are all part of human trafficking. But the 2013 case also shows how to mount a successful case, in order to see these horrific criminals put away.

This I know can be hard for prosecutors, especially when there is not as much evidence, unlike the above case. However, when we all work together, we can win in this fight, especially if we don't candy-coat the crime with terms like *sex offender*.

When you assassinate the soul of an innocent child or a broken woman, you are doing far more than making an offense. In fact, you are indulging in one of the most damaging of all crimes and human rights violations known to man. I often think of the three girls, now women, who were the victims in the above case.

Survivors know all too well how long it can take to heal and unravel the evil that was, by a miracle, endured. Each situation is, of course, different in many ways. But that much abuse and that much ugliness…more people need to understand: most victims of child sex slavery and human trafficking have experienced the extreme abuse and ugliness that those three girls experienced. I heard many people say that they felt even more sorry for the two girls in this case who were younger. This is an ignorant mindset.

I think this is because most people look at the circumstances of this case through their own opinions and ideologies. They simply have no comprehension of the extreme damage that takes place when anyone, at any age, is beaten and tortured.

As I have said, I think that the term *sex offender* should be removed from the criminal justice system. I believe that such terms soften the impact of the crime in the eyes of humanity. I think that *rapist* and *pedophile* and *child rapist* and of course *human trafficker* and *rape predator* are more appropriate. In terms of justice-seeking, I believe these terms will give the accused, the accuser, and the public a clearer depiction of the truth.

Even in moments of epiphany, years of prayer, day-to-day growth and coming of age, there is still work to be done to free us from the emotional and soul bondage that so easily takes place. For example, after years of thought-provoking prayer and counseling, a once eight-year-old victim of emotional abuse, now an adult, finally wakes up to the truth of who they are for the very first time. For example, someone finally forgives their mother for chasing Daddy away, after years of bitterness. The point is that they or we *forgive*; this happens when we become truly able to receive God's love and let go of all else. Forgiveness is one of the most difficult things to accomplish, especially after abuse and pain, but yet it is our greatest task. It is written and has been known through the ages that forgiveness helps us, even more than the person we must find strength to forgive. For, at some point, we all must be forgiven. Our God sees things from an infinitely higher perspective than ours; as we learn to trust Him and obey His guidance, amazing things begin to happen—within, through, and around us.

This is when we can *begin* to heal. What vile thing has been concocted in the hearts of so-called men and the women who say nothing, to think that a precious child of God desires anything but the love of God and the pursuit of a life filled with the blossoming of hope? A nation and a people can be destroyed by corrupting the minds of those who lead and those who will lead, starting with the potentiality of who they are destined to become. In this corruption lie the roots of human trafficking and modern day slavery. Its definition is given in the book, but its roots are even more important than its definition. I realize that it was in some of the root causes that I encountered and uncovered assistance—the assistance in discovering that I could live for the first time above the noise of my past, regardless of the symptomatic statistics given to me by the world regarding what my life would be like after having been what it deemed a "child/teenage prostitute" and profoundly "at risk." Sexual hate crimes—incest, molestation, trafficking, and rape—are some of the most psychologically damaging forms of crimes that anyone could experience.[5] That's what this book is about. It's also about knowing that God is faithful regardless of what has happened, and that it is only in His love and power that I've come to know and discover who I am—my preordained and destined identity.

Hearing His voice, following His lead, receiving His love, and loving Him back finally settled in my heart, and He taught me how to open and EMBRACE.

For the first time, I wake up giggling, sometimes dancing. My husband looks at me sometimes, as I just laugh and smile, as I am so filled with His love and simply happy to be alive. The awakening I experienced has unraveled His truth in me. I was once a victim, and some believe that we are never victims, but that isn't true. A victim is defined as "someone or something sacrificed or preyed upon."

That is exactly what happens, and sometimes survivors stay victims out of brokenness, and allow everyday challenges in life to cause them to feel victimized again. It is through discovery that we learn to grow and evolve from being heroic victims who survived something harsh yet remain broken, in pain, angry, confused, emotional, anguished, and lost, and move to freedom. Darkness tries to keep us in these broken states of being so that survivors do not become the thrivers they are destined to be. I pray that if you were a victim of human trafficking—or any form of sexual abuse, damaged by a destructive divorce, or in bondage to drugs, anger, hate, racism, or emotional abuse—that you are encouraged profoundly to learn how to live inside the rainbow of His covenant promises and purpose for your life.

1

HONESTY IS DIFFICULT WHEN WE DON'T KNOW THE TRUTH

"Darkness cannot drive out darkness; only light can do that. Hate cannot drive out hate; only love can do that."

Dr. Martin Luther King, Jr.
Renowned Civil Rights Leader/Activist,
Baptist Minister, Teacher, Author

And I, behold, I establish my covenant with you, and with your seed after you; And with every living creature that is with you, of the fowl, of the cattle, and of every beast of the earth with you; from all that go out of the ark, to every beast of the earth. And I will establish my covenant with you, neither shall all flesh be cut off any more by the waters of a flood; neither shall there anymore be a flood to destroy the earth. And God said, This is the token of the covenant which I make between me and you and every living creature that is with you, for

> **perpetual generations: I do set my bow in the cloud, and it shall be for a token of a covenant between me and the earth. And it shall come to pass, when I bring a cloud over the earth, that the bow shall be seen in the cloud: And I will look upon it, that I may remember the everlasting covenant between God and every living creature of all flesh that is upon the earth."**
>
> **Genesis 9:9-16 (KJV)**

"There is no greater agony than bearing an untold story inside you."

Maya Angelou
American Author and Poet

This is my story, with Scriptures woven in as best as the Lord allows. It is about starting what I call a "purity revolution;" Lord knows we need it and the true freedom which protects innocence and life.

How do you die, when you already feel dead? I had to ask myself this question that was born in my heart. This was difficult for me to do, but it is exactly what it takes to live a life with and in the love of God.

It is what is required of us, by the Lord; to die to self so that we discover who we really are. What would I ever have to give another, when I could not even take care of myself? This question would haunt me for years, until the answer was revealed.

I love rainbows; I always have. Rainbows are amazing and not always understood, by us, as to how they relate to nature. We see them in the sky, in oil slicks where there is water, reflected on our walls, in waterfalls, or in sprinklers. They occur when light passes through small drops of water and then bend backward totravel in the other direction. A rainbow is scientifically described as "an optical and meteorological phenomenon that is caused by a reflection of light in water droplets."[1] Scientists describe it as just that—science—and infer that rainbows are nothing special.

I remember seeing one for the first time, at least the first remembered. I thought it was the most magnificent thing that I had ever witnessed in the skies. Lightning, rain, even drops of hail couldn't compare to my first vision of a rainbow. It seemed to begin in a majestic place and land in the same. Scientifically, there is nothing unique or special or meaningful in their existence.

The same is said about the pregnancy and birth process of a healthy mother who knows that her child is special, or the innate knowledge that she has when one of her children is in danger or off track.

Or perhaps it is the times that we think of a friend with a certain strong impulse and they suddenly call, or we find that they are in danger. The fact remains: we are impelled to reach out! I love science and so much of what science has given us, as there is no greater scientist than God. He is the omniscient One, the Omni-science One.

God is the very definition of science and so wrapped up in all of who He is, as the Creator of heaven and earth and, of course, science. Yet sometimes scientists focus only on their science, not realizing that they are only starting to uncover what God is already aware of! That is where, in my love for God, I know that there is so much more to what scientists have uncovered and discovered. There is even more than we will probably ever know.

I am certain that many scientific *uncoverings* will lead to the power, promise and miraculousness of the Creator of the universe. It is written:

"I am the Alpha and the Omega, the Beginning and the End," says the Lord, "who is and who was and who is to come, the Almighty."

Revelation 1:8 (KJV)

Scientists and engineers also often explain the creation of airplanes without ever giving any noteworthy credence to the majestic enigma of the birds, eagles, and flying creatures which metal planes merely mimic. The evolution-versus-creation debate is a long story with a short answer. There may have been a Big Bang, but I know that God is the Creator and that His Word (Jesus), with wisdom by his side, was there. This is what Scripture says about wisdom:

> **"I [Wisdom] walk in the way of righteousness (moral and spiritual rectitude in every area and relation), in the midst of the paths of justice, that I may cause those who love me to inherit [true] riches and that I may fill their treasuries. The Lord formed *and* brought me [Wisdom] forth at the beginning of His way, before His acts of old. I [Wisdom] was inaugurated *and* ordained from everlasting, from the beginning, before ever the earth existed. When there were no deeps, I was brought forth, when there were no fountains laden with water. Before the mountains were settled, before the hills, I was brought forth, While as yet He had not made the land or the fields or the first of the dust of the earth. When He prepared the heavens, I [Wisdom] was there; when He drew a firmament over it, When He made firm the skies above, when He established the fountains of the deep, When He gave to the sea its limit *and* His decree that the waters should not transgress [across the boundaries set by] His command, when He appointed the foundations of the earth— Then I [Wisdom] was beside Him as a master *and* director of the work; and I was daily His delight, rejoicing before Him always, Rejoicing in His**

inhabited earth and delighting in the sons of men. Now therefore listen to me, O you sons; for blessed (happy, fortunate, to be envied) are those who keep my ways."

Proverbs 8:20-35

Prayer Corner

Dear Lord,
For us reading right now, let it be made clear that we beseech You with our whole hearts to give us wisdom as King Solomon asked for it, liberally and so freely! Lord, our God, give us this mighty wisdom that she who is wisdom may, according to your Word, be a master and director of that which You have given us to do. Establish Your good will and pleasure in the midst of what we do as we live and move in You, that we would be pure as You are pure, that we would shun evil and teach our children the power of love, the need to walk as You lead, Lord God! Not in a religious sense, but in the simple power of surrendering to Your will! Order our steps, Heavenly Father, and by Your Grace, through the power of the Holy Spirit, teach us to revive fully all of the supernatural wisdom in EVERY area of our lives, that we may prosper and be in good cheer!

*

I want to speak of the profound work of many of our pastors, evangelists, teachers, and lovers of God, especially that which our brother, Pastor Louie Giglio, has brought to our contemporary time with his *How Great is Our God* DVD series. This amazing series is a dynamic work on the story of creation as written in the stars and in the various galaxies (millions upon millions of galaxies in the known universe).

I have also learned some wonderful things by studying the sermons of Dr. Beverly "Bam" Crawford, much before Pastor Giglio's series was done, that relate to some of the scientific evidence in the cosmos. In addition, I learned from Dr. Carl Baugh of the Creation Evidence Museum in Glenrose, Texas, as well as Bishop T.D. Jakes in his sermon on "The Paradigm Shift" formulated by scientist Thomas Kahn.

All of this has blessed me and, I am sure, some of you with a leveling love and adoration. This evidence also points toward a God, even "Elohim Yahweh," who prepared so much for us in the universe that supported this tiny planet we live on, Earth.

Praise Corner

Praise you, Lord, for Your marvelous works! Praise You, Father, for You are and have done great things. Thank you for loving through us. We honor You in spirit and in truth for how You have given us so much, according to Psalms, designed it, all for Your glory and for your children. Praise you, Lord, that You have called us Your glory by calling us the Light of Christ—that You Father, love us that much to have died and defied death for us, oh God. We give reverence to You this day.

It is exciting to bless God and to know that He is in control! When we lean in to Him, He will deliver us. In many ways, He already has. My Bible tells me that when we are born from above we live in Christ and Christ in the Father. In the Book of the Psalms, God speaks through King David this way:

> **"He who dwells in the secret place of the Most High shall remain stable *and* fixed under the shadow of the Almighty [Whose power no foe can withstand]. I will say of the Lord, He is my Refuge**

and my Fortress, my God; on Him I lean *and* rely, *and* in Him I [confidently] trust! For [then] He will deliver you from the snare of the fowler and from the deadly pestilence."

Psalms 91:1-3

You see how amazing this is? Verse one describes a person who dwells by choice! We must choose to dwell in Him. In verse two, David chooses to declare, decree, and profess unto the Lord, "He is my Refuge and my Fortress, my God!" When we realize this *we* must declare it and in this we will notice so much about the blessings all around us—in HIM.

One of these blessings, for me is my joy of science, which is partially related to my uncovering of who I am and why we are here, but my fascination has existed since I was a small child. As a matter of fact, I longed to be a scientist. I had a chemistry set when I was seven years old, and it was my most precious thing. I had an unusual affinity for science and would often ponder how it all came to be and what else could be created from it. I thought that I had lost that dream, but I can see how God is even using that in my life now. No, I didn't become a scientist after all that has happened. Rather, I became an artist and one of His teachers, His children and ministers who, from the agonizing experiences from exposures to evil at a young age, have utilized my love for God. Or rather, He has melded His love for me and my love for science together, out of my early painful experiences.

Above, I shared about dwelling. But what happens when God's enemy, Evil itself, comes in like a dark, poisonous flood and robs a child of immediate destiny and the healthy growth of identity? How do we persevere and how do we trust again, to even begin to comprehend what is only possible with God? These are the mental health issues that tens of thousands of once innocent young ones deal with today. They are so deeply rooted in the subconscious that it is only our belief in the glory of God and the work it takes through Him that can uncover and heal our emotional and mental wounds. This is when wholeness finds its way into our midst. It is how it found its way into mine. I needed therapy and tons of help, but His divine wisdom, love, and presence was at the center of it all.

There are a few others in particular who have reached out to me who are under 13 years of age that need to understand His divine love for themselves, which gives us strength to fight and make sound decisions. Two, whom I mentioned earlier, were tortured and raped. Their perpetrator would take these two girls, along with two others in the home, lock them in a room, and sodomize and rape them repeatedly. He would also hang them from the ceiling by their ankles and cut them. As I mentioned, they often needed stitches, which were explained away by some accident of their own doing.

I realize that some may think it is easier to bear this with someone who is older. From my many speaking engagements and discussions, this is a general thought, but it's not necessarily true. What is true is that more people have mercy on the little ones and not the teenagers, and this is a horrible notion.

Often, abuse is even more shocking to older kids whose minds were beginning to process differently and did not see it coming. It is really astronomically painful at any age. Out walking and snatched. Thrown in a van. Beaten. Raped again and again. Filled with drugs and made to lay waste in a dark room with a pedophile or trafficker. At any age, this is unthinkable.

It was hard for me to believe after so much had happened that I could heal but, somehow, God has used all of the evil that I endured for His glory. Seems crazy, right? However, the process from there to here is a little of what I want to share with you in the hope that you will begin to heal, continue to heal, understand, advocate, and be aware regardless of what you have been through. Whether you are a victim, survivor, advocate, curious citizen, politician, leader, pastor, rabbi, or whatever, I pray that you will understand that what I am writing about is my story, my experience. This is what I know—firsthand—about the many grievous, destructive forms of bondage, about the massive social evil called human trafficking, and about the importance of freedom and love. We have issues with law enforcement and its understanding of a victim/survivor's trauma, and why many possible cases are thrown out. We need to discuss and learn so that our country will be revived, to believe in purity and respect for innocence. This is a purity revolution—one that declares that pedophilia, rape, incest, and gender-based violence are WRONG.

Purity is simple. Purity is knowing that children are innocent and emotionally full but mentally underdeveloped. It is in their observation of their environment (home, neighborhood) and world that they discover how life works, their part in it, and ways to develop their psyches. This encompasses their sets of values, goals and beliefs, not just about themselves, but also about you and the world in which they live.

We Were Born for Freedom, Yet the Enemy Distorts What It Looks Like

What happened in the garden, happens over and over again. Yet, I know we're smarter than that because the Word of God says,

> **"And afterward I will pour out My Spirit upon all flesh; and your sons and your daughters shall prophesy, your old men shall dream dreams, your young men shall see visions."**
>
> **Joel 2:28**

We just have to make the right choices, and we can truly do that only when we know who we are and, better yet, whose we are. When that does not work, when we don't know who we are, we must know who He is.

That's really the point of the fall in the garden: that we know who God is and that when we know, we will discover our life. The Lord desires us to die to self that we might live, so He can build us into His glorious temple of the Holy Spirit! After all, He is the mighty Architect. I realize and know that God in His mercy has built me from ruin, line by line, as a temple of His Spirit. What is so amazing is that He is the Master Builder, and when He is done, we become His masterpiece and He, our "Cornerstone" (Psalms 118:22).

Evil desires for us to stay dead and to keep us from being God's *masterpiece*. The wicked one works to keep us in that lost state which took place in the garden. Yet God requires us to die to self, so that we are born anew in Him. The enemy also works so that we never discover the truth but remain eternally lost. But God has given us the gift of life. Life, meaning the soul and the self, with the biblical definition being the vital breath, the breath of life, the human soul, the soul as the seat of affections; the will, the self, a human person, and an individual.[2]

I realize, in my own life and observations, that when we are with God He has, in His words:

> **"...made us sit down together [giving us joint seating with Him] in the heavenly sphere [by virtue of our being] in Christ Jesus (the Messiah, the Anointed One)."**
>
> **Ephesians 2:6**

This is literal, my friends! Our true self, our true life is found in God. However, we humans, we "earthen vessels," need certain things. We do not always realize that the simple needs are the most fulfilling over time, are those, which sustain our soul. Moreover, God, in His preparation for us, has made a way of escape from all the ills of life in order that He may fill us with all that we need to thrive and reign in life.

From physical needs to emotional and spiritual needs, He has all of the answers.

A supernova that falls from the eternal sky falls in pieces to the earth and is made up of the very unique minerals of which we, and even the food we eat, are made. I tell you, it wasn't until after I was whole again that I learned to appreciate the excellence of God's glory. In a great meal that is packed with nutrition, I've learned to see His love. It fills me with so much joy. Funny, huh? After all of the drugs and pain, it really feels good to be clean in Him. On many levels, girls like I was, during the era of my being forcefully trafficked, feel very unclean, and we don't think we will ever feel clean again.

"God created us to live with a single passion: to joyfully display His supreme excellence in all the spheres of life. The wasted life is the life without this passion. God calls us to pray and think and dream and plan and work not to be made much of, but to make much of Him in every part of our lives."

John Piper
Author, Preacher

I can tell you this: the deliverance from evil and the beginning of a new life created a burning passion in me that has a certain clarity and joy behind it—a "clarion call" that I can share, with the excitement of living, with others.

As I will share later, the brothel experience and the surrounding ills of it were ugly. There were girls in the brothel as young as 12. To see a grown man desire to urinate on them, and force even uglier, unspeakable acts on children is unthinkable. However, it happens every day. I was there, I saw it, and it happened. So I know that only a God, my Father, with His extraordinary way of being, could assist me and others in escaping, in healing, and, eventually, in excavating so much joy from pain.

At a symposium I attended at Johns Hopkins Bloomberg School of Public Health in Baltimore, Maryland, I met a doctor, James Mercy, Ph.D. Along with him, I heard people like Dr. Rebecca Campbell, Dr. Mohamed Mattar, and many in the fields of psychology, neurobiology, cardiology, and related fields of medicine. I also listened to organizational founders, community leaders, and other professionals. I was an invited guest, but I often speak at various events similar to this when not teaching at a seminar, prevention awareness summit, or church.

I do believe that we must share compassion and courage, so when I do attend events, teach, and/or share outside of the walls of the church, I find it exciting. I relate to all who come, with all that is in me; but it's not always easy.

Sometimes I have to lean in so deeply to the Holy Spirit to bring a wise message of heart, my own story, and be willing to open myself to an audience which holds many who do not wish to hear everything I would like to share. Getting up at a worship service in front of people who want to hear the name of God is much easier. It is also exciting because they came especially to get specific help, to be filled, whether they know it or not, and in the church setting we can pull out all of the stops! But this wasn't that church situation. So, while I was at this conference of medical and psychological professionals, I was so moved by their work involving the mind; while I was listening, the Lord kept having Scriptures and faith traditions flow and run through my heart, and I felt transported with emotion. The work of neuroscience that I had already been studying for about eight years or so was bursting inside of me. I was able to make new connections with the process of healing.

The Holy Spirit said, "Just ask a question," and I don't even remember the long statement I made or the entire question, but the participants were moved by it. I asked at one point about the victims who may be adults chronologically but emotionally were like children, in many ways underdeveloped. I know looks are deceiving and that many were, like I was, an adult child. What do we do for them, for women who have aged out of certain social services but are still in need? This and so much I said caused a palpable stillness in the room. After the session, 20 people came up to speak to me about what I did and who I was.

You see, God has a way by the Spirit of bringing the things we need when we need them—when we listen and do what He asks us to do, even if it seems simple. I saw myself asking the question and making the statement, even though I didn't desire to speak at all.

I have come to realize that when I feel it bubbling up in my spirit, the Holy Spirit is showing me what to do by His gift and presence in my life (Romans 8).

Nonetheless, Dr. Mercy, Dr. Mattar, and Dr. Campbell all spoke about the mind of a victim. As I said, I had been studying this for years already. God has given me a passion to teach and share—sometimes through my experience, sometimes via the Scriptures—the process of my own journey and how I made it through all of the ills to discover who I am and was meant to be. Dr. Mercy was very helpful, and he asked me what made the difference in my healing. I responded in kind:

Dr. James A. Mercy, Ph.D.,
Special Advisor for Global Activities, Division of Violence Prevention, National Center for Injury Prevention and Control, Centers for Disease Prevention and Control

Dear Dr. Mercy:

Thank you! You asked me, "What made the difference?" In a word...or three...Love, Hope, and Stamina. I can break that down in a neurobiological form and, trust me; I do try in my book to some degree. But what we need to understand is the power of love and hope in action, not man's measure of it but that of the Divine, the One that created heaven and earth. Saying this, the brain is always working, even when the diversity of the soul, personality and response of each individual involved in extreme vile trauma varies. However, the human desire to thrive is innate and natural. Thus, in time the love of those, whose action has reached in and shown us how to hear from the point of purpose and seemingly impossible destined dreams revealed in our hearts, shows us that we have a chance. More than that, we begin again, one day at a time and then, if we faint not, we awaken. I was waking up to the truth of who I was from the moment I intended to live; it was merely a matter of direction and stamina until, one day, I looked back and laughed about the paradigm shift that had been evolving over time. And frankly, I still do.

Love, Light,
Brook Parker-Bello

I would long, as many do, to know how much I was really loved—one of my deepest desires. I longed to know whether I simply *belong*ed, and whether God was not only real but actually had me on His mind, in His thoughts. If he cared about my very existence and me at all, then indeed I could belong. I would attempt to understand how this love was able to unravel the long and tangled web of deceit that plagues the heart and mind. God showed up for this very reason to rebuild that which was lost and to "Announce release to the captives." (Luke 4:18)

It is exciting to realize that He came to set us free in the totality of our Being: our thoughts, feelings, perceptions—our entire outlook on life, regardless of how old we are and what we've survived. I longed as a child and adult to know more. Even if I did know, I could not describe it or know how to express it, at that time. Although I was not after any nostalgic pot of gold or mystical destination at the end of my covenant rainbow, I would eventually discover that I was only after what it stood for. That was and is the supernatural love of God and the power in that love which included all that He has to offer us. The Bible warns of the many individuals

"Having a form of godliness, but denying the power thereof: from such turn away."

2 Timothy 3:5 (KJV)

I was empty, and I realized this was a good thing because I could now be filled; and so can you. I didn't have to worry about a "form of godliness" because I didn't have anything and I knew it. I also could discern those who may have had that form, those who pretended to love me but didn't. Do you know how many girls I mentor who were child sex slaves and also members of a church, temple, or other religious organization? Or how many of the rapists or traffickers were pastors or leaders in the Church, or esteemed community leaders in high school, university, or prestigious professional circles? You would be shocked; but I have seen this evil, firsthand.

I was broken, sadly humbled, and regarded as lowly—regarded as nothing by many. You see, I desperately needed the power of God and did not have a thought to deny His power. And neither should you. But I needed it to be all that the Lord came, died, and defied death for me to be and become in the first place, and so do you. Regardless of what we face, He has made a way for us. He is the "Way-maker"!

The kind of power and love that could erase the deep pain I felt and give me a reason to live, to fight to live, was what I longed for.

And if I could find it and somehow be bold enough to receive the covenant that we have been given when we are born from above, as the seeds of Abraham in Jesus the Christ, then I could truly live inside the rainbow. If I could do that, then I could live not by what the world sees or by its dictates, but by His very breath, wind, and glory. I could even dare to live by His Word and then I could somehow begin to see that, as the Spirit wills, miracles,

> **"signs, and wonders" would follow me as a believer.**
>
> **Mark 16:17 (KJV)**

Look, if I were going to go for this thing, I would want to go all the way. And if the Lord says I can, I will, and I am able, in Him—then who am I to say He's wrong? After all, He is the Christ, the Christos, the Anointed One, the Son of God, Son of Man, the Prince of Peace, and the only one who died for me and then defied death. Amen!

This death and life of the Savior, which I had to learn to partake of in my own life, eventually helped me choose to leave off living a dead and downtrodden life. This enabled me to rise as He did, rise in Him from the ashes of my old life, to be reborn in the new life that He was and is so overjoyed to show us.

After all, God calls this journey the "Gift of Life."

*

There are many reasons why we could second-guess the existence of a God who loves us, who cares about our personal issues, even the day-to-day ones, and our very lives. I cannot say that I was not one of those doubters at one point or another, even though as a little girl I believed in God. It was only as I grew *into the distorted and destructive world around me* that all of these reasons arose, which for a long time damaged my innocent faith.

Yet eventually I learned that all of those reasons that pulled me further from the truth were false. There were and are far more reasons to live fully and freely in God, I believe. And this proved that the trauma I endured and the world-induced false skepticism could not, in fact, affect me any longer, in the way that I had long allowed it. After all, I also discovered that the foremost and best things in life are free; at least, I find this to be so. Perhaps this is why we don't give these free things the true value they deserve. But someone paid the price for the freedom we rarely live to experience to the fullest. And the price that was paid has a value far greater than I ever fully understood...until now. Jesus is that value, and He paid that price. Scripture reads:

> **"After this, Jesus, knowing that all was now finished (ended), said in fulfillment of the Scripture, 'I thirst.' A vessel (jar) full of sour wine (vinegar) was placed there, so they put a sponge soaked in the sour wine on [a stalk, reed of] hyssop, and held it to [His] mouth. When Jesus had received the sour wine, He said, 'It is finished!' And He bowed His head and gave up His spirit."**
>
> **John 19: 28-30**

Halleluiah! Oh, Exalt the Lord with Me and Let's Praise His Name Forever.

The Savior *gave up* His Spirit to God the Father and we, in turn, do the same when we are born from above. Incredible, isn't it? A miracle right there! What an awe-inspiring picture of the truth; how can it be denied? Christ and our faith settle the matter and rest it, and us, in His loving hands.

That is also to say, the truth of the meaning of my life I have just discovered.

I have become acquainted with some of this freedom, which He came, died, and rose for me to have. Sometimes I could just pinch myself! If I said I get all of it, I would be wrong. The Church: a body of believers who have not even tapped into the "tip of the iceberg" of all that God has for us and what we are capable of in and through Him, of which I had only bits and pieces of discernment before. He said:

> **"And the Ever-living One [I am living in the eternity of the eternities]. I died, but see, I am alive forevermore; and I possess the keys of death and Hades (the realm of the dead.)"**
>
> **Revelation 1:18**

Jesus defied death for us, which means that at some point I would come to understand that His sacrifice would associate death to my past as well, and that is exactly what I needed to know, including all which that death had authored within my soul, heart, and mind. Knowing Him as I do now, this actualized the fact that my past and derelict soul would have to be extricated, overhauled, rewired, and transformed. To allow this, I would eventually have to learn the truth about who the Lord God designed me to be.

"Make a pact with yourself today to not be defined by your past. Sometimes the greatest thing to come out of all your hard work isn't what you get for it, but what you become for it. Shake things up today! Be You...Be Free...Share."

Steve Maraboli
Author, Motivational Speaker

This is what we all need to know at some point in our lives. In the Book of Romans, Apostle Paul writes:

> **"Do not be conformed to this world, [fashioned after and adapted to its external, superficial customs], but be transformed by the [entire] renewal of your mind [by its new ideals and its new**

attitude], so that you may prove for yourselves what is the good and acceptable and perfect will of God, *even* the thing which is good and acceptable and perfect [in His sight for you].”

Romans 12:2

IT IS GOOD TO BELIEVE GOD

It is so good living on this side of hell—the outside of it. It was indeed Hell—to be so in despair and bound up from trauma as to want to end my life. And I tried, over and over again—through drug addiction, induced seizures; I would inhale freebase cocaine and then have my chest hit so hard that I would experience a full blown seizure just to *feel* the high.

I planned my death so clearly that I became physically ill one evening after being on the set of the film “The Last Warrior” the month before, violently vomiting and dry-heaving in the midst of having just come in from doing yard work on my new home, as I thought of a million ways it could be done.

I was up for six days straight, so high on cocaine that my heart was pounding like thunder inside my chest as I lay on the floor, feeling like skin and bones. I was full of so much agony, hopelessness, and sadness that I felt my life had no real or measurable value—that I was ugly and not smart enough to survive.

I felt so unclean because of the sex slavery and rape, the repeated attacks and the psychosis all of this causes; and because of that, I felt unloved by those around me. I had a hard time even understanding what love looked like.

Outlook on simple cultural norms such as watching the news and even reality is different when one is abused because how we define things is often from the point of our own brokenness.

On the other hand, I had a vision of this amazing planet and universe that was meant to be a gift. I did know that somehow, even through us human beings as God's caretakers of the earth according to the Scriptures, that there must have been hope somewhere.

However, I still thought that I must have ended up on the wrong side of the tracks—the side where many often told me I wasn't lucky enough for that hope. But what has God to do with luck? What has destiny and purpose to do with luck?

> **"And the Lord God took the man and put him in the Garden of Eden to tend and guard *and* keep it."**
>
> **Genesis 2:15**

Therefore, *eden* or our version of it here and now is a place, a garden, where I believe we see its splendor in the glory of life itself and in the wondrous things God has created. We are created equal and cannot judge our future or God's love for us by what happens along the way. We must judge it by the blood of the Lamb that was shed for us and love and live forward in that power.

Conversely, we also experience and see great evil, and if we end up on the wrong side of it through whatever circumstance, we must cry out and get the help we so desperately need.

I could no longer care that I was screaming and crying out at church or which eyes were watching me cry out, sing too loudly, and shout, "Amen!" because I needed to be saved after all that happened in my life through sex slavery, rape, and abuse. I thought there must have been some huge, crazy misconception. Where was the beauty in my life except in the parallel universe everyone *else* seemed to be living in? I was affected by the abortions I had and what psychotherapists say about those who have abortions. What they cause in a female's heart and mind is a long list of pain-related issues that can affect her state of being on a myriad of levels, which are sometimes not experienced until much later.

The fact is that I can have no children now; it's perhaps too late, even after a recent surgery to fix things that were broken back then. No babies could come from my womb because of the damage done, which I say is now healed by faith and the surgery (of course, with God all things are possible)!

I felt guilt and shame for finally desiring to heal from it all and discovering my purposed, my preordained identity in God—only to hate myself for not doing it sooner!

I had lost time and the innocent beauty of what I saw as a child when I played "explorer" in my backyard.

It seemed so far away.

I was a once straight "A" student who was told that my high school completion was a joke, even though when I picked up my scores from the local community college the receptionist said, "Wow, you scored high; you should go to college." But I thought at that time (with my distorted visual perception, brokenness and prison mentality) that I heard only a patronizing tone, as many of us do when the darkness is taunting our spirit.

I've often thought about the fact that there are prisons we imagine when we envision criminals, and the prisons they dwell in when they are caught. There are many actual prisons here in the United States of America. The United States of America is a federal constitutional republic consisting of 50 states and a federal district with some of the most notorious prisons in the world. If you commit a crime, you may have a special reservation with a single bed and a barred view of unseemliness. Famous prisons include Rikers Island, Leavenworth Federal Penitentiary, the Louisiana State Penitentiary, Folsom State Prison, Sing Sing, and San Quentin State Prison, just to name a few. Believe it or not, they aren't the most notorious. The most overcrowded and tenebrous prisons are those that are invisible, and we live in them more often than we think.

"If you should see a starving man standing with mouth open to the wind, inhaling draughts of air as

if in hope of gratifying his hunger you would think him a lunatic. But it is no less foolish to imagine things which only inflate it without feeding it

Bernard of Clairvaux
French Author, Monk, M.D.

After being trafficked, I am certain that I looked like that lunatic. These prisons that I did and many others do experience are not built with brick and mortar, they are not built with the conscious plans of locking anyone inside, per se, at least not by the ones who live in them. The spirit of darkness builds them. And, with our help, they are built by the back-slapping, do-it-yourself kits in our culture which frequently suggest that if you work, do the daily grind, moil, push, and trouble hard enough you will find a decent level of bliss along the way. But is this true; is this hope?

I longed to understand the following Words of God as I looked back and began the conscious journey to wholeness, the journey from my own prison. The following Scripture would eventually resonate deeply within my heart:

> **"Except the Lord builds the house, they labor in vain who build it; except the Lord keeps the city, the watchman wakes but in vain. It is vain for you to rise up early, to take rest late, to eat the bread of [anxious] toil—for He gives [blessings] to His beloved in sleep."**
>
> **Psalm 127:1-7**

Even if you choose not to know or seek God, and if God is true to His promise to never give His children more than that which we are able to bear (1 Cor. 10:13 KJV), then could my point of view of myself and the world around me be counterfactual? Even after I became a believer in God, I could never have anticipated, until now, that eternal life begins *now*, before it happens literally in heaven.

Maybe I think too much and maybe, just maybe, in our innocent and pure desire to know God fully, He even answers such questions and encourages, even enjoys our quest to know Him more.

The Book of Hebrews states:

> **"Therefore then, since we are surrounded by so great a cloud of witnesses [who have borne testimony to the Truth], let us strip off and throw aside every encumbrance (unnecessary weight) and that sin which so readily (deftly and cleverly clings to and entangles us, and let us run with patient endurance and steady and active persistence the appointed course of the race that is set before us."**
>
> **Hebrews 12:1**

That word *cloud* means an atmospheric phenomenon,[3] a "cloud of witnesses" already gone before us, like a mighty, sweet presence of love and support, proclaiming that we are not alone by any means. When I think of running the race, I think of, "Where?" Which brings us to our gate, the gate that we need to walk through—that I needed to walk through. Could the "narrow gate" be a lifestyle, a way of seeing that those who are not going through it are not the ones that give you the genuine clues to life? We do learn from all people and all situations, but I learned the most from love.

Perhaps there is a type of collective blindness to the true reason for our existence, and sometimes we as believers have tried to live by trying to please the world to the point of not pleasing God. What I meant is, I think *I* was trying to do that for a long time. It's true.

People full of faith are very important to God and are how He shares grace from His heart through ours toward others, and gives us answers to some of the biggest problems in our world today, including modern-day slavery, human trafficking, and the grave evil victimization of women and children. I'm not speaking of those who do not walk in love, are not teachable, and don't care or show that kindness to all people everywhere. I'm speaking of those who have seen and experienced the love of God and can't help but share it.

The thing is, we can do great damage to the kingdom of darkness. The Bible tells us:

> **"Enter through the narrow gate; for wide is the gate and spacious and broad is the way that leads away to destruction, and many are those who are entering through it. But the gate is narrow (contracted by pressure) and the way is straitened and compressed that leads away to life, and few are those who find it."**
>
> **Matthew 7:13-14**

The narrow gate consists of the kind of pressure that it takes to generate in us the understanding of powerfulness, of how to utilize the ability we have by the Holy Spirit.

The Bible says in the Book of Acts:

> **"For in Him we live and move and have our being; as even some of your [own] poets have said, For we are also His offspring."**
>
> **Acts 17:28**

I believe that as we move and have our being in Him, we *move through that narrow gate by moving in Him.* Furthermore:

"And ye are Christ's, and Christ is God's."

1 Corinthians 3:23

And if we are Christ's and Christ is God's, then we are meant to go through this extraordinary piazza: a place where we are confronted with the meaning of life and the questions as to what to do next, especially after bad things happen to us or we do bad things that we have come to terms with. Apostle Paul himself walked through that gate after being a murderer—even worse, a serial killer. He was able to receive all of God's gifts and blessings for his life; in turn, ours have been filled with enormous gifts and blessings for all.

The narrow gate, this passageway which Paul, Peter, Mary, and others walked through in ancient Rome, is the road to victory. It is like walking and watching our Jesus along the Via Dolorosa in Israel, as He carried the cross amongst the spitting and violent garrison, down the pathway like the mighty and gentle "Rose of Sharon" (Solomon 2:1) and the "Prince of Peace" (Isaiah 9:6).

He was subjected to extreme wickedness for us. Yet with all the evil and hard-to-imagine terrible sin that we would ever witness or do, when we receive His gift of deliverance and allow it to revive our soul, we can still come boldly in love before Him and reign in life. I was there in Israel and walked along it, and I thought of how it might have been back then. I realized that we get to ride through this place with our ticket and full fare paid, gliding in beneath the wings of the Almighty because He took the abuse, the spit, the cutting crown of thorns, and the ultimate agony on the cross—all for us.

Thus, the rod and staff that King David speaks of in the Book of Psalms as we walk or run through the narrow way guides us through it, when we say yes to God's will. I would eventually choose life, not knowing what that would mean or the process of what had to take place until much later.

> **"The LORD is my shepherd; I shall not want. He maketh me to lie down in green pastures: he leadeth me beside the still waters. He restoreth my soul: he leadeth me in the paths of righteousness for his name's sake."**
>
> **Psalms 23:1-3 (KJV)**

As the Spirit of God wills, we can do God's will within our households, our lives, our communities, the lives of others, and in the world, in miraculous and loving ways. That is what the narrow gate is about to me; it is about setting captives free, healing the sick as the Spirit wills, feeding the hungry, clothing the naked. It is about providing education, funding missions creating organizations, and supporting those who are caring for others and working to bring about justice for all.

It is about kingdom building and basic human rights for all. This was actually the kind of stuff that I thought of as a little girl, like many children, and then it was robbed.

Look, the term *teenage prostitute* is an insane phrase brought about by a blinded culture. How could raping a child ever be considered anything but what it is—rape?!

How could the world be anything but the flip of a coin, with no hope, when it is destined to die?

Could a dying world be that death, is now, the process of the rebirth of life in many areas, as long as we are the ones that realize it, and let go of dead things in the process? For example, the way that we are being born anew in Christ, including the earth itself is going through the same undulating good and chaotic changes that do now and will ultimately lead to Zion, that will have obviously great beauty, as it is written,

> **"For the Lord will comfort Zion; He will comfort all her waste places. And He will make her wilderness like Eden, and her desert like the garden of the Lord. Joy and gladness will be found in her, thanksgiving and the voice of song *or* instrument of praise."**
>
> **Isaiah 51:3**

God's love leads us ever forward; His love did lead me as I let go of the past and dead things and began to say yes to what could be. The New Jerusalem will be, just as we are to be, born again, born anew.

> **"And I saw the holy city, the new Jerusalem, descending out of heaven from God, all arrayed like a bride beautified *and* adorned for her husband"**
>
> **Revelation 21:2**

The process and journey that I have taken and am taking until the return of the Redeemer and/or my departure or transition to heaven has to be one filled with the understanding of how loved we really are. This had to become a mainstay for me, even when everything else around didn't appear to speak of that love.

There is a reason we are here when we are, and I needed to know what and why that was; but back then, in my dark era, some very hard and crazy times of sabotage began to get worse. Broken people break things and I broke many good things in my life.

How can anyone stand next to individuals in judgment, assuming they believe they are "all that," simply because they have money, or are pretty, or they seem puffed up, when all they might feel is shame, loneliness, and the profound effects of sin and guilt?

I was at a table read for the film *Strange Days.* I played Cecile, Angela Bassett's sister. I did not really understand what was happening, having not yet been healed or dealt with the abuse, trafficking, and rape that I suffered. I had not had any therapy or told anyone about it at that time. I was in shock to walk into a room with actress Angela Bassett, Ralph Fiennes, Juliet Lewis, and the amazing director, Kathryn Bigelow. I looked up to all of them, especially Ms. Bigelow. I froze; I wanted to cry right there and pinch myself. Could this be real? I sat down and was introduced to everyone. I was shaking, and they probably could tell I was freaked. I came off like a quirky artist, I guess.

There was a scene in the film where I, as Cecile, was driving in a car on New Year's Eve. I remember being so excited, I took a real camera to the set and began snapping pictures in the car. I mean, I really lived it! I was never reprimanded to my face, even though that was not something that one should do, but for me, I had really become the character.

Yet I, Brook, was so overwhelmed that I ran with it; I imagined what it would be like to have a sister who loved me and fought to protect me as the pretend one did in the film. I even snapped a flash right in Ralph Fiennes' face. I don't think he liked it much, but I didn't seem to care at the time; I was just excited to be there.

Angela was very cool about the whole thing, and I think she saw it as a "creative choice." Looking back, I think she had a certain insight to some degree about what I may have been feeling. But the thing is that on the set, I was good while working, but I did not know how to relate to people outside of that.

I had understood only that I was nothing, so I responded to things with the attitude that I had done something wrong; I was always on the defensive. I was grossly intimidated and felt it was my job to try and be perfect and bring order where there seemed to be none.

Victims of various forms of abuse often react this way; I know I did. We heard that Ms. Bigelow's father had died. I remember feeling so sad for her, but I could see her strength on set and wanted to do my part to make sure things were done in order. I wanted to be perfect, because in being perfect, no one could see that I was damaged.

That is how traffickers/pimps train you, and that is how I was "groomed." And this is flat-out Evil, to cause a child to grow up in such a way as to question, as I did, my importance in the earth, sabotaging a child's whole life out of F.E.A.R.: "false evidence appearing real."

I naturally felt that it was my job to make things better. Take someone who was born to serve as a creative person, crush that vital spirit with violent, repeated rape and verbal and physical abuse, submerge the bewildered and traumatized child into a toxic life of sexual slavery. The result is a person with a distorted, slave-minded, submissive, having-to-please-others-all-of-the-time mind set. The false identity that abuse creates has all the ingredients of a bomb: an explosive mixture that is detonated by certain trigger impacts. This caused an out-of-balance state in me.

I accidentally said things about a boy who was sick on set. I had met his mother at the table read, and she took a liking to me and asked me to look out for him. I felt I should watch out for him, so I did. He asked for my help on set because he felt dizzy, and after that I said and did things that were not mine to do or say regarding what kind of treatment he needed. But he came to me crying, and I had a heart to protect. I still do love to seek care and justice for others, but now I understand protocol and boundaries. It doesn't mean we can't operate with compassion; we just have to respect the process depending on where we are.

I broke protocol, something I did not understand at all at the time. This can also be true even when someone else is doing something we think is out of order. I was completely oblivious to this snowball effect of sabotaging all that I had been doing little by little. Even though the brokenness is not our fault, I want adolescents and all others to know that, ultimately, we are still responsible for much of the outcome of our lives. We have to fight and find the way of escape out of mental torment, but obviously we cannot do it alone. And it is not always our fault when we don't, based on the damage at the time.

For instance, you may not know or understand that God really does see inside of our hearts. He often states in the Scriptures various truths about the heart and mind: "…let this mind or (heart) be in you that is in Christ Jesus" (Philippians 2:5);, "If there is among you a poor man, one of your kinsmen in any of the towns of your land which the Lord your God gives you, you shall not harden your [minds and] hearts or close your hands to your poor brother" (Deuteronomy 15:7).

The words for *heart* and *mind* in Greek and Hebrew are often the same; therefore, God <u>leads</u> us to our destiny of healing when we follow Him. However, He also states that people fail because there is no intercessor, no one who stands in the gap.

Thus, as the called-out, the body of believers according to the Scriptures, we must pray for and with one another so much more.

The poor don't just hold out their hand for money, but the poor, also those with humble heart (which we all must be—of humble heart) are often afraid to cry for help. They're holding out their hands for life, for the life they see others have, even when it's not perfect! So, when we pray and intercede, we are reaching out to them and to our God.

We are also surrendering to the Holy Spirit, and when we surrender <u>all</u>, we will be led by the Spirit of God, and,

> **"For as many as are led by the Spirit of God, they are the sons of God."**
>
> **Romans 8:14 (KJV)**

The Lord is able, through relationship with us, to share unknown mysteries, words of wisdom, words of knowledge and encouragement from the throne with those who need it! Some people say that we don't need to pray long, and that may be the case, but this refers to thanking and requesting. In relationships, we need to spend time to cultivate the bond we have with the Lord and the Holy Spirit through being still, praying, worship, studying, and reading the Word, especially out loud, as well as listening and sharing with Him.

The foundational views of any healthy and close-knit relationship are the ones where those involved spend quality and quantity time together.

I love to read the Word out loud. God begins to share intimate mysteries, answers to prayer, prophetic declarations, and all manner of amazing things. They are birthed from spending time together with God. The sound our voices carry declares who we are and what we believe in the realm of the Spirit; it is wonderful. As the evil spirit said in that day,

> **"And the evil spirit answered and said, Jesus I know, and Paul I know; but who are ye?"**
>
> **Acts 19:15 (KJV)**

If we plan on doing anything for God's kingdom, it's good for many to know who we are and what we believe.

That being said, we need to know who we are, and this treasure is the one thing that is stolen from so many.

"I have held many things in my hands, and I have lost them all; but whatever I have placed in God's hands, that I still possess."

Martin Luther, Doctor of Theology

2
LOVE, HOPE, AND STAMINA

The Greek word for encourage is "parakaleo," and the word for the Holy Spirit is the Word "paraclete." The NAS New Testament Greek Lexicon, Strong's Number 3870, definition of this word has a great lexical reach that also translates to *encourage* or *comfort.* Other meanings are these: to call to one's side, call for, summon, address, speak to (call to, call upon), which may be done in the way of exhortation, entreaty, comfort, instruction, and so on.

What is also exciting is that Webster's describes the definition of "paraclete" as the Holy Spirit. In Middle English paraclyte, from Late Latin paracletus, paraclitus, from Greek paraklētos, literally, advocate, intercessor.[1]

These words are the same—one being the verb to encourage, and one being the noun, the person of the Holy Spirit, the Encourager or Comforter. So as we pray in the Spirit, we should pray in our native tongue in the understanding also that God will reveal so much more about His Kingdom, His children, our lives, the world in which we live, and our place and purpose in it. I see my work as a ministry of encouragement in many ways, as it is what I always needed to get past the trauma I've suffered.

Isn't that exciting, knowing that just a simple word can alter the life of another? I know that those kinds of words, the Words of

God, which are Jesus Himself, have saved my life from the pit, from pain, from suicide, and from a living hell. The Lord says,

"He exalts His Word above His name!"

Psalm 138:2

God is truly awesome! You know, over time the Gospels have brought a perpetual healing that, along with cognitive therapy (speaking and being listened to and seeking wisdom), helped me to understand basic boundaries. I was transformed! I realize that it was not an instantaneous healing, but it was a supernatural process.

The joy in this is the story of the landowner written in the Scriptures:

> **"For the kingdom of heaven is like the owner of an estate who went out in the morning along with the dawn to hire workmen for his vineyard. After agreeing with the laborers for a denarius a day, he sent them into his vineyard. And going out about the third hour (nine o'clock), he saw others standing idle in the marketplace; And about the eleventh hour (five o'clock) he went out and found still others standing around, and said to them, Why do you stand here idle all day?"**
>
> **Matthew 20: 1-3, 6**

The story in Matthew 20 is powerful, and too long to quote here, but at the end of this parable, when Jesus describes His kingdom of heaven, He says,

"...the first shall be last and the last shall be first."

Matthew 20:16

Our Savior rights wrongs, and in creation itself, there is a supernatural balance to how our Heavenly Father has created the heavens and the earth, and all that is therein. You see, whether they worked for only one hour at the end of the day or all day long, their wages were the same!

Not only does this signify eternal life based on whenever we come to the Lord and believe in His name, but also that through Him, we are cleansed from ALL unrighteousness, through His redemptive power and the gift of salvation (which means wholeness, right-standing with God, and righteousness as we stand before God and man unashamed).

It also signifies the immediate "daily benefits" written about in the Psalms. When we turn to Him after whatever has happened, whether to us or through us, we are redeemed and our lives made new!

What that means is that even though I got a late start in life after healing from child sex slavery, what would have taken me years to accomplish in what is perceived as the appropriate journey (or to reach a certain destination, planned goal, educational passage of time to achieve this desire, this career, ministry, or dream, which to me are all intertwined), He does it, and it happens rapidly and even exponentially with a supernatural and heavenly momentum

The New Testament says:

> **"Nevertheless, do not let this one fact escape you, beloved, that with the Lord one day is as a thousand years and a thousand years as one day."**
>
> **2 Peter 3:8**

This verse was so encouraging to me because without this, what was I to do? Thanks be to God, we need not concern ourselves with such matters. All we have to do is say *yes*, and take the first step right into His loving arms! One of the most important things for my life was to learn and to understand the basis of relationships. A lack of this understanding sometimes means you can discredit authority whether you understand it or not, because when you are broken, you often don't know the difference. I didn't; and as you read more of my story coming up, you will see this was true for me. It is written,

"...the wisdom of man is foolishness to God."
1 Corinthians 3:19

When we don't operate with God's wisdom and operate in "sense and reason," we open up and give authority for the spirits of darkness to wreak havoc in our lives. I did this often as a broken and unhealed soul.

Dictionary.com describes the realm of the ego as "the 'I' or self of any person, a person as thinking, feeling, and willing, and distinguishing itself from the selves of others and from objects of its thought." This can often get us into trouble when we take ourselves too seriously or operate in selfishness. In psychoanalysis[2] it is "the part of the psychic apparatus that experiences and reacts to the outside world and thus mediates between the primitive drives of the mind and the demands of the social and physical environment." But to live a life of freedom we must learn to not only understand earthly environments but we must *hear* the Divine.

All that the ego is, at the core, is an extreme focus on self. So, regardless of which end of the spectrum of the ego we find ourselves on (or I was on) when we are out of balance with the love of God, we are still trapped in the realm of the ego, which is merely self-focus. This is true whether one is on the narcissistic end of the spectrum, the low-self-esteem portion, or even the brokenhearted low, low end.

The ego of self-focus and self-centeredness, which is far too consumed with its own needs and feelings, leads many astray. Taking my eyes off myself was pivotal and a big portion of being able to hear God on matters of healing for myself and those I serve at More Too Life or around the globe..

Feelings—ugh. I was so concerned about what people thought. The evidence of my concern was that I was afraid to be with others and when I was, I just knew that I was doing something wrong.

I wasn't dressed right, or the very thoughts in my head were wrong—for certain they were out of order; or I said something wrong, or wore the wrong perfume and by some crazy coincidence someone just happened to be allergic to it, and I felt that even that was my fault! I was very uncomfortable in my own skin.

> **"The heart is deceitful above all things, and desperately wicked: who can know it?"**
>
> **Jeremiah 17:9 (KJV)**

> **"He who leans on, trusts in, *and* is confident of his own mind *and* heart is a [self-confident] fool, but he who walks in skillful *and* godly Wisdcm shall be delivered."**
>
> **Proverbs 28:26**

I eventually discovered that I was not my brain but that I am spirit and have control over my brain and my thoughts.

This is how understanding my thoughts and what I choose to let remain on my mind, or what I choose to "cast down," has become a key process of transformation in my life. But note that these uneasy experiences are part of the stepping stones that lead to God's glory in our lives, if we allow it. I learned that a synonym for *ego* is the word *mind* and that we truly are not our minds, or our brains as I said before, but the *observers* of them. Once I learned that, and practiced it, I could then learn not to condemn myself every waking moment of the day with guilt—the guilt we often find ourselves living in. Jesus died to free us from that very same guilt.

Because of the bad decisions I made after trauma, and the lifestyle trauma created for me, I was no longer who I felt I had been inside as a small girl. I began to notice that I had a lot of hang-ups, such as crippling fear, anxiousness, and low self-esteem.

That's how I often felt on the sets of films and TV shows I worked on. At events I had to attend, I would muster up enough nerve to go but would stand in a corner just watching the world pass by.

I did not know who I was, but I knew I was afraid of my own shadow and had a hard time leaving my apartment. I knew that I wanted and longed for someone to listen so I could feel safe enough to open up and tell someone what I had gone through. I longed to trust someone enough to say I thought I was losing my mind, or at least what I thought was my mind.

How can so many walk in judgment against others when we have not walked a mile in anyone's shoes but our own? But when you think about it, even in that, it is not always our own shoes as we often copy the world around us, without ever even discovering who we really are. Problem is, we rarely discover this truth.

Well, since it is true that we are not perfect, and since the Word of God teaches us from the story of the alabaster box (Matthew 26:7) that we will come to know and love so much more weighted to how much we are forgiven, then God has given us an amazing hope. Now, even though it was not my fault as a little girl, there would come a time when I would have to forgive those who hurt me.

There would come a time for me to release the anger, because all of that anger would keep me in bondage to unsoundness, egotism, drug-addiction, and many other behavior and personality disorders that now are treated with Xanax, Prozac, Valium, and other drugs. There would come a time when I would have to forgive the most difficult person in my life, and this is usually the hardest for us all, and that is the self: myself.

FORGIVENESS

Of course, at the time I had a feeling in theory that forgiving others was a good deed, but I knew in my brain that this had nothing to do with the violence that so many innocent women, children, and even adult males suffer in the world.

I assumed that murder, rape, pedophilia and similar evils NEVER fall under that "good deed" of my theory of forgiveness, until I learned that God doesn't require good deeds.

Nor is He mocked, even though it seems I tried to mock Him. He only gives each of us things to do that have a way of perpetually, in a forward motion, in an astronomical supernatural power that I cannot explain, give us transcendence from the flesh and transform us to experience a peace of His eternal understanding.

> **"Therefore my heart rejoiced and my tongue exulted exceedingly; moreover, my flesh also will dwell in hope [will encamp, pitch its tent, and dwell in hope in anticipation of the resurrection]."**
>
> **Acts 2:26**

What a profound taste of His awesomeness! We know that as Jesus honored the woman who understood that only a crumb from the Master's table, if it is in fact from the Master's table and considered only fit for the dogs, was wrapped in the warmth of His love and power. Because if in fact it was from His table, it was full of His blessings if partaken in faith; and I have spent much of my life eating these very crumbs and was honored to do so. However, I still enjoy the whole loaf as well. It's all in our perception and perseverance in and by Him. Even the same glory that raised Jesus Christ from the dead was and is so much more than I believe the human brain and this side of heaven can fully comprehend.

This is what the Lord shared with me: He told me that I'm a prisoner when I hate those who hate me—those who have shown their vile hatred by their actions toward me.

On the other hand, when I do not lash back, I am not a prisoner.

This does not mean I cannot have a righteous anger and fight in love against injustice. It just means that vengeance isn't mine.

I am free when I love those who hate me. If I ask the Lord for forgiveness but have not forgiven others, my very life and future divine accomplishments are hindered. It is not to hurt me that I forgive, nor do I have to live with or ever even see these persons again. It is simply a matter of healing my heart.

Now I could begin to understand love and trust, even for the first time, in my everyday life. Scripture states:

> **"Come to terms quickly with your accuser while you are on the way traveling with him, lest your accuser hand you over to the judge, and the judge to the guard, and you be put in prison. Truly I say to you, you will not be released until you have paid the last fraction of a penny."**
>
> **Matthew 5:25-26**

This Scripture is extraordinary, because what I see in the Spirit, in my prayer closet, when God speaks, is that if we do not come to terms (forgive) with the accuser (those who hurt us), then we continue to live out and perpetuate this same spirit of accusation and darkness (unforgivingness). And it will eat away at God's Word in our heart and keep us from discovering Him and His ability to operate in His love for us and through us.

At the same time, our own hearts and minds (because of transgression and guilt) will keep us in bondage to lies, and we will not have a clear conscience.

I don't know about you, but I had no choice.

This bondage is in *our own* life and *our own* skin, and if and when we wake up to the fact that it's there, how much time will we have wasted? As much as I did? Because I was not to live in my own skin (flesh) or my own life (self, will). I was to "lose my life" so that I could find it.

That kind of prison, as the Scripture states, does not allow release until "we pay every last penny." (Matthew 5:26) How awful does that sound? I knew that I could not afford it. In my wildest of dreams coming true, I still would not be able to pay what was needed to dissolve all of what took place at man's creation in the garden, and even in our own lives, which is why there is so much sin in the world to begin with.

But we already know that's not right, to have to pay, even though many have tried, which is why God "sent His only begotten Son." He paid the price for us, and when we receive Him, we receive all He has for us. And that's a promise; that's His promise.

Look at what verses 44-46 state about freedom from this:

> **"But I tell you, Love your enemies and pray for those who persecute you, to show that you are the children of your Father Who is in heaven; for He makes His sun rise on the wicked and on the good, and makes the rain fall upon the upright and the wrongdoers [alike]. For if you love those who love you, what reward can you have?"**
>
> **Matthew 5:44-46**

The Word even teaches us that "he loads us daily with benefits." (Psalm 68:19) It is something we receive on a daily basis, as there is no greater Father than God. I would even learn later to begin to try and understand to lean on and trust in Him. If you can do this, He will release His supernatural power in your life as He did, and still does, in mine. "His ways are higher than our ways," and it doesn't always make human sense, I know, but it is good sense. And you know what? You don't have to look around to see if anyone notices. As you move, it will be discovered as treasures often are.

*

"To be transformed, our job is to 'behold'—to continually contemplate—God's glory, focusing our spiritual gaze not primarily on things like Christian duties or our unworthiness, but on God's spectacularness."

Dwight Edwards, Author

The following account in Scriptures is a depiction of how Jesus can take the broken, damaged, assassinated soul and bring a deliverance that cannot be explained. Glory to God for His faithfulness!

This Scripture follows the passage where the woman anoints Jesus' feet with perfumed oil from the alabaster box. You may recall the story: the men in leadership standing about accused Him, saying that if He were really a prophet He would not let this woman whom they called unclean touch Him. But Jesus came especially for her, just as she was. He came to set the captives free,

> **"And Jesus, replying, said to him, 'Simon, I have something to say to you.' And he answered, 'Teacher, say it.' 'A certain lender of money [at interest] had two debtors: one owed him five hundred denarii, and the other fifty. When they had no means of paying, he freely forgave them both. Now which of them will love him more?' Simon answered, 'The one, I take it, for whom he forgave *and* cancelled more.' And Jesus said to him, 'You have decided correctly."**
>
> **Luke 7:40-43**

"...for unto whomsoever much is given, of him shall be much required." (Luke 12:48) We are given redemption, forgiveness, deliverance, a new life, and a new birth. Praise God! We are loved so much, and all we are truly required to do is to receive it...and rest in God's presence after we do. This is the fight of the ages, to understand and know that the Ancient of Days has you protected. He has protected me beyond my ability to discern.

I would like to tell you how and when I first received the Lord, along with some other amazing things that have given me a "new lease on life." I began to realize that since Jesus loved me as much as He loves you, maybe I could through Him, find a way to be strong enough to move forward and "taste and see" (Psalm 34:8) for myself that the Lord is good. Eventually, I did just that.

> **"Be strong, courageous, *and* firm; fear not nor be in terror before them, for it is the Lord your God Who goes with you; He will not fail you or forsake you."**
>
> **Deuteronomy 31:6**

Isn't it wonderful to know that, through Jesus and what He has done by defying death on the cross, death to all of the ills in our lives has already taken place and all we have to do is recognize it? All we have to do is say *yes*!

I began to realize that life is truly good; it is such an immaculate gift and cannot be anything but! Look at this place, this planet, the sky, the seas, mountains, valleys, and hills. Look at the flowers and grass, the fresh herbs, the birds of the air, fish, and wild beasts, along with the food: vegetables, fruits, nuts, and all types of fresh meats and cheeses. God has given us a glorious planet. A supernova falls to the earth, this brilliant star, and in its womb are the particles of which we are made. All the planets in our galaxy, upon the billions and billions of galaxies in the known universe, point to us, provide for us, minerals and life—even the dust of the earth from which we are made.

> **"The heavens declare the glory of God; and the firmament shows *and* proclaims His handiwork. Day after day pours forth speech, and night after night shows forth knowledge."**
>
> **Psalms 19:1-2**

WHAT KNOWLEDGE DOES HEAVEN SPEAK OF?

Surely God's glory lovingly spoke to me: that I was planned, that my life was planned and foreordained for receiving His best! Victims of human trafficking, forced into prostitution, labor, domestic servitude, child sex slavery, with all the horrendous sexual violations and abuse, need to know that they are loved and full of potential, regardless of the horrors and damage they have suffered. They need to know that their past does not have to dictate their future!

My baby words can't express the depths of the celestial, divine love that God has for us.

Psalm 19 also speaks about who He is, His character, His artistic, joyous, loving, compassionate personage. I let His love fill my mind and heart with radiant joyousness every day. I desire that you allow God to fill your heart and soul with His wisdom, His presence and His divine blessing for your life.

What I long for you to see, what I long for you to understand, is that you are loved beyond compare just as you are!

Prayer Corner

Dear God,

Let the words of my mouth and the meditation of my heart be acceptable in Your sight, O LORD, my rock and my Redeemer, as this little book shares. Oh, how I love Thee, You who have set me free!

3

LIVING INSIDE THE RAINBOW BEGAN DURING MY JOURNEY THROUGH HELL

From the Word of God, written in the Scriptures, it is clear that being in bondage exists on many levels. For me, it would take a long time to understand the difference. The differences among the various forms of bondage in the world, which are often formed at early ages, are why it is so important to help young children, growing minds, and willing adults to truly not give up on God's creation, 18 years and up!

In His unique creation of the mind and heart in us, we all have the ability to change; we have the ability, through Him, to allow the illumination of His glory and light to alter and change our very nature. I discovered that the many forms of bondage in the world— narcissism, various forms of idolatry (such as sexual symbolism, drug addiction, love of power, and all forms of lust and extreme greed), gossip, fear, criminal activity—all have their roots in the prince of the lower instincts, the material world, evil itself.

The United Nations Protocol for Human Trafficking states

trafficking is: "…the recruitment, transportation, transfer, harboring or receipt of persons, by means of the threat or use of force or other forms of coercion, of abduction, of fraud, of deception, of the abuse of power or of a position of vulnerability or of the giving or receiving of payments or benefits to achieve the consent of a person having control over another person, for the purpose of exploitation."

Today, a slave is not necessarily a person in chains or shackles. Slavery is not simply ownership of one person over another. Modern-day slavery can be much more subtle. People are enslaved not only through physical restraint but also through coercion, fear and intimidation.

In today's global economy, victims can be enslaved by being runaways who are too young to understand and are enslaved by forced drug addiction, by threats of deportation, by lack of viable alternatives, and especially by debt or false employment tactics. It took a long time for me to understand that being free from abuse, homelessness, drug addiction, and sex slavery did not at all mean that I was acquitted.

> **"But this is a people robbed and plundered; they are all of them snared in holes and hidden in houses of bondage. They have become a prey, with no one to deliver them, a spoil, with no one to say, Restore them!"**
>
> **Isaiah 42:22**

What did this mean for me exactly? Did my accidental self-emancipation mean, I wondered later, that time had healed me, that I was out of the snare of darkness in holes and hidden houses of bondage? Did it mean that I was no longer a "spoil", with no one to say, "Restore her?" I guess what I mean to ask myself is, was I free? Was I let loose, liberated, let off the hook, released, and absolved? The pure and simple fact of the matter is that I thought

I was. It did not matter, it seemed to me, that I was suicidal, drank too much, secretly loathed myself, was crippled by fear and living a life of homosexuality or lesbianism that I knew I didn't long for, or enjoy. It's really the same thing. The word *homosexuality* can be used for male or female, such as "mankind," whatever you want to call it. I knew, personally, I wasn't born that way, even when others tried to tell me I was. I liked men but was too frightened to trust them, too afraid to let myself love what had always seemed to bring me nothing but torment.

I would go through several so-called female companions, from models to actresses, seeking relief from the trafficking I had suffered, before I understood that that wasn't me nor who I longed to be. Life seemed rooted in lust and other times in pain. That homosexual life, as I experienced it in those places, was rooted in lust and brokenness.

Many of the ladies that I knew disliked men, were hurt by them at some point in their lives, didn't trust them. That is not so different from *some* of the homosexual men that I've met who didn't like women. They may have liked to impersonate them at the clubs I would attend, but they would also tell me all that they didn't like about women.

I have had many homosexual male friends who were also kind and sweet. But there are certain men, homosexual and otherwise, whom I have seen turn on women; it was the most horrible scene I witnessed, and the most hate I'd felt, not only toward me, but toward one another within that arena.

Unfortunately, I have also found that many pimps/ traffickers I knew were homosexual, bisexual, or on the "down-low," a newer slang term that describes men who are outwardly heterosexual but secretly have sexual relations with other men. Not to say that all homosexual men are that way, but the fighting and pain that I have witnessed in their presence with their lovers is some of the worst hate that I have ever witnessed but whether gay or straight, hate is hate, as I also know that heterosexual couples have killed their so-called lovers as well, married and unmarried.

My best friend Dale who died of AIDS was homosexual and the only male school friend I felt truly loved me back then. I really miss him. We met when I was a young teen and shortly after we met, his sister shot herself in the mouth. I was with him often after that. He would see me when I was with The Trafficker and not know what to do because he was in a similar situation. I loved Dale and still think about him often. There were so many older men that pestered and used him in his young brokenness, when all he really needed was a father.

You see, younger people are so desperate for leadership and loving mother and father figures, they will, like I did, take it in distorted ways, and end up in a bad situation. Especially when they are hurting and the pretend father or mother figure really seems to love them at first. But what the abusers were really after, with Dale and me, was to "season," "groom," and then sell us. To prostitute us.

I remember walking into a gay club after I was out of the trafficking prison, trying to find a life. I had been familiar with them because The Pimp and Madam who trafficked me the first time would bring me to an adult gay bar with a fake I.D. The Madam was bisexual, and I remember that in that club, the emotional darkness was strong, and everyone wanted some form of sex and partying.

There were even hardcore S&M guys there who would invite me to parties, but it was not the kind of party where a child should be, let alone anybody for that matter.

But later on, we were at one of these clubs again with some girls, and it was the same; people looked at us like we were new, fresh meat. They were prowling; and because I wanted love, I was trained to accept it, even though I dreamed of being married, loved, and having children.

Unfortunately, I had witnessed my mother, who is a beautiful woman, being hit and beaten up by men at an early age. I could see that she also needed and desired to be loved so very much but often was in sorrow, because she did not get the love she really needed as a child. She is so smart, ahead of her time in many ways. I believe, however, that due to the deep and harsh upbringing she had to endure and fight through, and there for her, she did not know how to mother me in the way she would have desired.

*

Honestly, I could say that most men, at that time, brought me nothing but profound heartache, as a child and girl, through repeated rape, physical abuse, emotional vituperation, and some of the most disgusting, evil, and wicked things that have been done to me and to others I once knew. Now I work with many of them, in our restoration and life discovery plan.

I will give what I consider a light example. To tell you the ugly details of anything more is not important.

I remember a time when I was stripped of my clothing, beaten, and made to squat in a dirty bathtub and act like a dog. I wasn't allowed to leave the empty bathtub or the position until I had learned my lesson and was able to listen to the words over and over of how I was made for nothing, useful for nothing, and was subject to that pimp/trafficker's torture, @#$%^&* (the words are too foul to repeat).

There were other times when I was made to repeat that I was crazy, and I would not be released from the chokehold until I repeated it.

I would later be afraid to go into public places or parties of any kind unless I was high. I thought I had to prepare in order to go to a simple outing. I was so gripped with fear that only getting high (narcotics and very hard drinking) seemed to help.

There was no one saying to me, “Be restored,” and at the time, I wasn't saying it either. I didn't think that anything was wrong with me but me. I thought that the fears and thoughts of suicide, the nightmares and the vivid dreams that somehow came to pass , were because I was not healthy somehow. At the same time, I believed that everything bad about me was because that was how I was supposed to be. I surmised that it was simply how I was born.

LET GOD BE TRUE

> **"What if some did not believe *and* were without faith? Does their lack of faith *and* their faithlessness nullify *and* make ineffective *and* void the faithfulness of God *and* His fidelity [to His Word]? By no means! Let God be found true though every human being is false *and* a liar, as it is written, That You may be justified *and* shown to be upright in what You say, and prevail when You are judged [by sinful men]."**
>
> **Romans 3:3-4**

How could I be honest when I didn't know the truth—the truth of who I was really born to be after all that I had been through?

The anguish of not knowing became part of my journey through hell. How could I learn what it was? That's why we are to let others know as believers! We are to be unashamed of the Gospel, for it truly is "sharper than any two-edge sword" (Hebrews 4:12). It truly defeats foes and fills us up with the power of God which is found in His love. I longed for someone to share with me, but I think they thought I had it all, so no one really tried. Oddly enough, there are a number of cults, really weird ones, that tried with an intense passion to get me to believe in some very odd things. There were even religions—and I say this to emphasize that Christianity is not only a religion but also a way of life—that tried to say that there is no God. However, I know that the Lord was here always, even before the foundations of the earth, as He is the professed Word of God, who became flesh and dwelt among us!

> **"In the beginning [before all time] was the Word (Christ), and the Word was with God, and the Word was God Himself. He was present originally with God. All things were made *and* came into existence through Him; and without Him was not even one thing made that has come into being."**
>
> **John 1:1-3**

Thus, in *knowing* God, I would eventually come to understand. That is what I long for you, or someone you know, or someone whom you will meet or minister to—to know that God is real.

His omniscient personhood is the most real thing that you will ever encounter, and even when you think you've encountered it, it goes all the deeper. When you find it, you will find life for the first time.

I have also come to understand that my life—my pain, all of the anger and revenge I longed for, the forgiveness as well as my future hopes and dreams—would have to be lost. How could I do this and not get the feeling I was losing my mind; it seemed too spiritual for me, too radical, too much?! But herein lies the audacity of faith and trust in action.

> ***"For to be free is not merely to cast off one's chains, but to live in a way that respects and enhances the freedom of others."***
>
> Nelson Mandela - former President of South Africa
> South African anti-apartheid revolutionary

I'm not a scientist, but I will explain my journey of the study of the mind and how I healed, as I understood this science and my passion for it at that time. It made alive for me some of God's Word as the Lord in the Scriptures often refers to our heart and mind. It's now common knowledge that a child's brain doesn't fully develop until 24 years of age. The process of how the neurological dimensions of the hemispheres and connections of the brain grow during this time frame is crucial to who we become. For me, my mind, brain, and heart were wired at a significantly horrific time in the architecture of my life.

They were formed by the abuse that I saw growing up and that I experienced by the traffickers who brainwashed and raped me during my coming-of-age journey.

However, as you can see, the "coming of age" has different meanings as we look at the truth.

The true coming of age cannot happen without the love of God and the Holy Spirit. So, in my understanding of the brain, I have learned the following: "Thoughts and memories look like trees and are called neurons or nerve cells, because thoughts are the result of what we hear and read and see and feel and experience. This means that whatever you <u>grow</u> is part of you; actual branches in your brain that create your attitude and influence your decisions"[1]

Not only this, but it is like our soul. My soul had to be excavated, and a rewiring of it was done by the brain's neuroplastic abilities. These are the "brain's ability to change as a result of experience and cognitive exercises, thoughts and so on.

"These changes can occur as a result of learning new things or because of damage to the brain. Up until about 40 years ago, experts believed that changes in the brain were only possible during infancy and childhood, but research has demonstrated that the brain is capable of altering existing pathways and even creating new ones."[2]

I realize that the Lord had already made this available to us and why and how we truly can be "transformed by the renewing of minds" (Romans 12:2). There is a profound order to things which cannot be explained. The Bible says, "…we spend our years as a tale that is told." But look at this:

> **"For all our days [out here in this wilderness, says Moses] pass away in Your wrath; we spend our Years as a tale that is told [for we adults know we are doomed to die soon, without reaching Canaan]."**
>
> **Psalm 90:9**

Moses speaks of the fact that they were still in disobedience and ingratitude and that, in that state of consciousness, their lives would remain so. That makes good sense, because we know that there will be an end to evil, to the roots of bitterness, and to the creation of all that is born from sin. But Love, who is a person (The Elohim—Triune God), is without end. When we walk in this love, the only love, and all else is an imposter, our possibilities in this world and the one to come are filled with supernatural and divine life, beauty, and endless possibilities. Even in this life, with its chaos, it can be and is, with God's help, a victory.

> **"Blessed (happy, enviably fortunate, and spiritually prosperous—possessing the happiness produced by the experience of God's favor and especially conditioned by the revelation of His grace, regardless of their outward conditions) are the pure in heart, for they shall see God!"**
>
> **(Matthew 5:8).**

> **"Weeping endures for a night, but joy comes in the morning"**
>
> **(Psalm 30:5).**

A night season is temporary, and I longed to get through mine, which seemed to me to last far too long. One of the meanings of *pure* is also *authentic*, and I longed to get to this, to my true self in Him.

It is the lie of the ages to rob us, through abuse and other forms of sin, of the authenticity, of who God created me to be. It is only in being who we were uniquely called and born to be that we will truly live in His joy—which is, in fact, being made pure in Him. When we are pure in heart, we will see God! Not just later, but now and throughout all our lives, our affairs, and whenever we need Him—even when we don't think we do.

"Whenever we find ourselves on the side of the majority it is time to pause and reflect."

Mark Twain - Author

It is incredible how the times we live in seem to be more adverse and difficult than previous times. Some people refer to "the good ole' days."

I surmise that in every era there are great things and not so great. Regardless of what time it is or what age we are living in, God has prepared "a way of escape." We are to locate it for ourselves in our very lives and times. This was so very difficult for me, and I am sure for many of you, but there is still a way of escape. I found it only by buckling down in the Word of God, as well as with therapy and much prayer and meditation on His love. I also found it in serving others, and in enjoying times with friends, scuba diving, and hiking—did I say therapy/cognitive practices? As I'll share often, I also found it in learning how to rest and abide in Him, over time. When we do not know who we are, our lives are absorbed into our environment, and, let's face it, sometimes our environments are toxic. The Bible tells us that

"bad company corrupts good judgment."

1 Corinthians 15:33

What about a childhood or a lifetime of bad company? The evil one is a lie, a prevarication, a complete and utter falsity, and moreover, he is a defeated foe!

Isn't that what the darkness does? He tries to destroy God's people, often before they have time to grow into who they are supposed to be. This includes not knowing God, not knowing the great "mustard seed" potential of who we are, surely not knowing the Holy Spirit, and to top it off, not knowing how to get to these.

That's what abuse causes, what grave sexual slavery, rape, and molestation do: they cut to the core and the lost, never-known identity.

Purpose is then hidden, exploited, and buried in the depths of our hearts. Some are so lost that they often merely imitate what they think living is but are actually living in a type of hell or a prison.

I have mentioned before that the word for *mind* in the Greek is *heart,* and that science has discovered that the heart is in fact a sort of mini-brain. I often share this, because much of a life compromised and damaged by trafficking and sex slavery truly is a battlefield in our heart and mind, our soul.

In the Greek Lexicon, Strong's number 2588, the word for heart is the word cardivan or cardiac, which is the word for our heart organ and also the same word for our mind, soul, and emotions. The KJV New Testament Greek Lexicon gives this definition for heart: "the centre and seat of spiritual life, the soul or mind, as it is the fountain and seat of the thoughts, passions, desires, appetites, affections, purposes, endeavors of the understanding, the faculty and seat of the intelligence of the will and character of the soul so far as it is affected and stirred in a bad way or good, or of the soul as the seat of the sensibilities, affections, emotions, desires, appetites and passions."[3]

At the same time, the heart communicates with the hippocampus, the elongated ridges on the floor of each lateral ventricle of the brain.

This section of the brain is thought to be the center of emotion, memory, and the autonomic nervous system.[4]

I believe that the subconscious mind is at the center of the heart. Even Scripture with its use of the words *heart* and *mind* together interchangeably, gives us this very picture.

I will speak more on this later. My pastor has often taught that the subconscious is "the realm of the supernatural."

For me, this is that deep-within point of who we are, the "oceanic plates" of our heart where we can actually shift to choose life or death.

It is where painful memories are stored or seemingly lost, as well as good ones.

It is where our very own born-again spirit speaks to us, after the Holy Spirit speaks to it. We are, after all, spirit, soul, and body and thus hear in different ways from God who is life. We also hear from the evil one who is death.

But always by the Spirit, even when we hear God audibly, as I have. I wonder if the spirits of darkness understand anything about the human body and the functions of it. Lucifer or Satan must have been studying it since the time of creation, after all.

Once a person is physically out of bondage, it does not mean they are free. Slavery is a state of mind, and human trafficking (modern day slavery) causes bondage in one's total existence. One has to be freed in many ways.

Once again, some words used to define human trafficking are: transportation, transfer, harboring, receipt, threat, force, fraud, coercion, abduction, deception, abuse of power, vulnerability, payments, benefits, exploitation, debt, and so on.

The words describe to me what happens beyond the smoke screen, the same old ills to imprison our souls (our will, mind, and emotions).

Once we are out of the physical prison, recovery is more about the mind than anything else.

"Indeed, the safest road to hell is the gradual one - the gentle slope, soft underfoot, without sudden turnings, without milestones, without signposts."

Screwtape
Character from C.S. Lewis'
The Screwtape Letters

The devil has not used anything new. Some people say, "New levels, new devils!" Just because it rhymes doesn't make it true, because there are no new devils, only one, Satan or Devil, in charge of a whole legion of fallen angels or demons.

The demonic is no joke, and there are many forms and types of evil (call it what you will)—unclean, wicked spirits, and they are all under Satan. We may face different demons at different times, but there is only one devil.

The Bible says the enemy barely bruises our heel (Genesis 3:15). The blood of Jesus the Christ, who took the keys and set captives free, has achieved the victory, even for us!

The current times, compared to the Word of God, describe what Satan has always done and is still doing. Now, there are even more distractions to try and keep us from discovering who we really are in God. I was distracted by pain, and after the pain it became everything else. I'm not saying I wasn't a victim. I was a victim, but no one stopped and said, "Be restored" (Isaiah 42:22). Many cannot or could not see that by the Spirit I and often other victims of abuse are not operating in a personality or identity that is ours in the first place. Neuroscientist Dr. Caroline Leaf writes, "How distorted is your thinking? Are you forming a personal identity around for example, a disease?"[5] I realize that I was formed during and after my experience as the enemy tricks us, and I didn't even know it. This is often true with many who have been tortured and abused! So, the journey, I believe, took longer than it could have, but even in that God has made a way to redeem the time, for all of us. That being said, intercession is so very important. It is also important not to assume that people are okay just through our superficial judgment calls about how someone looks, what cars they drive, where they live, and how they dress. The Bible tells us

> **"Man looks on an outward appearance but God looks at the heart."**
>
> **1 Samuel 16:7**

This is the case when we judge someone we think is not attractive or distinguished at all. He may be the most stunning person around or she might have the most beautiful voice we have ever heard. We can miss inexplicable truths when operating in such a way.

We often miss our very own value, beauty, and the wonderment of who we are by judging others and ourselves by outward characteristics. I believe that people thought I was okay because of the way I dressed and looked, but inside I was literally dying, screaming for help. But no one I talked to really took me seriously. They assumed that I was "being emotional" and could get over whatever was ailing me with time.

SO I KEPT UP THE FACE UNTIL I HAD A NERVOUS BREAKDOWN

The Scriptures tell us that God has said: "Yea, truth faileth; and he that departeth from evil maketh himself a prey: and the LORD saw it, and it displeased him that there was no judgment. And he saw that there was no man, and wondered that there was no intercessor: therefore his arm brought salvation unto him; and his righteousness, it sustained him (Isaiah 59:15-16, KJV), which is why I had to write this book and why I started *More Too Life* and one of its initiatives and themes, *Living Above The Noise;* which means above the chaos and noise of life, and with starting More Too Life, with nothing to go on but His passion within me. But it was all that I needed to begin.

One of my favorite lines from any film is taken from *The Usual Suspects*: "The greatest trick the devil ever pulled was convincing the world he didn't exist." Thought-provoking, don't you think?

I remember, just after the first time I was raped, the man left quickly. I knew that if I told anyone about it, he would hurt me and that my family would be in even more trouble. But what I didn't realize as a young child is that the fear of him hurting me more, or of my family not believing me, didn't compare to the years of calamity and chaos that keeping quiet, would cause my heart, mind and life.

Unfortunately, a large percentage of victims don't tell because of the judgment and discrimination they experience, along with mistrust of the imbalanced and sometimes biased judicial system as it relates to prosecution in sexual violation, rape, and pedophile cases. As children, the confusion lies in our young minds, thinking it was our fault, that we sinned or did something bad and that is why we were hurt in the first place.

Darkness will always try to capitalize on all kinds of sin, whether committed or experienced, which is transgression and guilt.

> **"Be well balanced (temperate, sober of mind), be vigilant and cautious at all times; for that enemy of yours, the devil, roams around like a lion roaring in fierce hunger, seeking someone to seize upon and devour."**
>
> **1 Peter 5:8**

My 11- or 12-year-old body ran to the bathroom and doubled over on the floor, confused and in pain. I was bleeding and there was this stuff coming out of me. I didn't know what it was, and I was in terror. What did that grown-up almost 30-year-old man have to do with me kissing a boy on the cheek in my fifth grade class? A mere peck, that lasted all of a millisecond?

I honestly hadn't learned about any of this, nor did I realize until a few weeks later that this pedophile had robbed me of something that I would never get back. I didn't understand that I had lost what is most precious to a young girl and the woman that I would be one day: my virginity. An unlocked sacred place, when violated, is an extraordinary loss. It is also just as precious to a young boy or man, but men don't teach this, which is part of the problem.

I had already changed after the rape. My desire to climb trees and play with a sweet and explorative quality ended. My young womb was robbed and pillaged of its purity. The moment I discovered that I no longer was a virgin, I felt dead and confused all the more.

The nightmares that I had suffered as a child became worse. A fear of the dark and of my own shadow began to overtake me, I was just a kid and my life changed. Even in this, though, God had a plan and a "way of escape."

> **"Therefore, [there is] now no condemnation (no adjudging guilty of wrong) for those who are in Christ Jesus, who live [and] walk not after the dictates of the flesh, but after the dictates of the Spirit. For the law of the Spirit of life [which is] in Christ Jesus [the law of our new being] has freed me from the law of sin and of death. For God has done what the Law could not do, [its power] being weakened by the flesh [the entire nature of man without the Holy Spirit].**
>
> **Romans 8:1-3**

I have come to understand that if we are not acquainted with the love of God, it is difficult to know the profound and beautiful truth of why we are born and who we really are. Or, might I say, who we were designed to be, even with our individuality and one-of-a-kind uniqueness.

"For God so loved the world that He gave..."

John 3:16 (KJV)

Don't forget, we read earlier that Jesus is the Word, and the Word is how we create in thoughts, then in action or deed.

This is a powerful truth in that Jesus is the Word, the Logos that God used when He created us and everything else in the inception of the universe. Whether it was a big explosion of creation mixed with God's Word in a whisper or a shout, the point is that we are here and that God is real! Halleluiah! For His love is from everlasting to everlasting even if we do not know, according to Genesis 1, how long "God hovered over the earth" before the seventh day rest at creation. Regardless, before that began, God hovered.

> **"In the beginning God (prepared, formed, fashioned, and) created the heavens and the earth. The earth was without form and an empty waste, and darkness was upon the face of the very great deep. The Spirit of God was moving over the face of the waters."**
>
> **Genesis 1:1-2**

> **"God said, 'Let Us [Father, Son, and Holy Spirit] make mankind in Our image, after Our likeness' So God created man in His own image, in the image and likeness of God He created him; male and female He created them."**
>
> **Genesis 1:26-27**

There is so much to these words of God, some of which we will look at later on. However, what I realized as I traveled more and more along the journey of being whole is that the Lord is the Word of God, and since God used His Word to create, and because we are in the image and likeness of Him, we can do the same! We have dominion. The Bible says we have the victory! Our heels once again bruise the head of the enemy, so that we may live and move in the Lord and have our being in Him.

> **"For in Him we live and move and have our being;**
> **as even some of your [own] poets have said,**
> **For we are also His offspring."**
>
> **Acts 17:28**

The Word of God says that by our words we are justified and by our words we are condemned. We choose (Deuteronomy 30:19) in how we think, in what we say; we can choose life or death; we create all around us and in us. This is not—and never was—*a secret* but God has made it known to us right here and all along. Jesus may have come in the flesh only just over 2,000 years ago, but He was with God from Creation as His Word that became flesh.

> **"In the beginning [before all time] was the Word (Christ), and the Word was with God, and the Word was God Himself. He was present originally with God. All things were made *and* came into existence through Him; and without Him was not even one thing made that has come into being."**
>
> **John 1:1-3**

This is why I sought His help at a temple that was not a church, and why, after months of deep prayer and meditation, it was Christ our Lord who showed up and taught me what freedom really meant. (I'm still learning, of course.)

Just the simple power of an ultrasound, if you've ever had one, tells us of yet another awesome thing in creation. An ultrasound can literally see inside the body. These sound waves permeate the surface levels of the skin. The more water in certain areas of the body at the time of the ultrasound, the better the sound waves work. The body is 65 percent or more water, the same as is the earth God has created,[7] and drinking water is key to living a long healthy life in ways that are exponential (I will go into this in a forthcoming activity journal to this book).

But the fact is that, according to God in this text,

"water is the Word."

Ephesians 5:26

To have this water, this Word of God, permeate our very life, we will be living a worshipful life: a life rooted and grounded in His love, which is a life of destiny. This was exciting for me after all I had been through, after all I had witnessed; and as my eyes were opened, I needed to understand how to share hope with others! Mark 11:22-23 says, "And Jesus, replying, said to them, 'Have faith in God [constantly]. Truly I tell you, whoever says to this mountain, 'Be lifted up and thrown into the sea!' and does not doubt at all in his heart but believes that what he says will take place, it will be done for him.'"

Hallelujah! I could be transformed and be freed from the mental and physical soul assassination and anguish in which I lived.

Once free, free enough, I could share how God did that for me—and He can do it for you!

What is more exciting than that? It makes all else seem futile in comparison because, Scriptures say:

> **"All things were made *and* came into existence through Him; and without Him was not even one thing made that has come into being. In Him was Life, and the Life was the Light of men. And the Light shines on in the darkness, for the darkness has never overpowered it [put it out or absorbed it or appropriated it, and is unreceptive to it]."**
>
> **John 1:3-5**

That is amazing. You mean that all things came through the Word of God? And God did not make anything without Him? That in the Lord is and was life and that life, my light? And my light shines in darkness, and this darkness has not overpowered it, and the Lord has allowed our light to be His very life? His love is such?!

How was I supposed to know that or even comprehend it? Nobody told me. How was I supposed to discover that after all that I had endured? After people urinated on adolescents for their perverted "pleasure"…how are we supposed to know that God is real? How was I supposed to know that, when husbands and wives would pay for us to watch them beating one another? How was I supposed to know, when these people who enacted these perversions looked like cuddly, Oxford-wearing, white-linen-adorned, White/Black/Asian, nice-car-driving people with plush, long blonde hair, who made you think of fresh-baked cookies and golf? How, after we young girls were forced to hit them and watch them in their bondage say to us, "Harder and harder," to the point of their skin welting and bleeding—how was I supposed to realize there was a way out, even once I was out physically? We had to be so drugged-up to do this.

But I still remember the sadness on one side of the wife's faces and the wickedness on the other, as though they were stuck. It was like they were different people within one. It was the demonic at work, and I was face-to-face with it. I was just a kid, then a young lady, then a lost woman-child, with no one to say, "Restore."

These days, rape is one of the most prevalent crimes in America, with 25 percent of American females being raped. "The U.S. Bureau of Justice Statistics states that 91 percent of rape victims are female and 9 percent are male, and 99 percent of rapists are male. One out of six U.S. women has experienced an attempted or completed rape. More than a quarter of college aged women report having experienced a rape or rape attempt since age 14 with 1 in 5 girls on a college campus in the USA will experience rape, we need to stop this. Some types of rape are excluded from official reports altogether (the FBI's definition, for example, used to exclude all rapes except forcible rapes of females), because a significant number of actual rapes go unreported. In addition, a significant number of rapes reported to the police do not advance to prosecution.

As well as the large number of rapes that go unreported, only 25 percent of reported rapes result in arrest. Many rape kits are not tested. Only 16 percent of rapes and sexual assaults are reported to the police (Rape in America: A Report to the Nation. 1992 and United Nations Populations Fund, 2000a). Factoring in unreported rapes, only about 5 percent of rapists will ever spend a day in jail. From 2000 to 2005, 59% of rapes were not reported to law enforcement. One factor relating to this is the misconception that most rapes are committed by strangers. "[8]

Rape is a violent, dark, foul crime of soul assassination, mostly executed by criminals that have forgotten or never knew that they were made to physically protect and serve others more frail than they were—and, to serve God. These very men who do not understand are the very ones who "split hairs," claiming that some rapes are forced, others are unforced. For the record, all rape is rape. Thus, all forced!

I was a tiny, skinny little tomboy who loved to climb trees, play with animals, and help my mother in the yard; who loved to sing, and to play explorer. Many 11 or 12 year olds look eight, and I was no different. I didn't know what sperm was, nor had I ever seen a naked male. At this point, I did not even realize where the male organ actually went. I had kissed a boy, as I said earlier, that year in the fifth grade for the first time. Or should I say, pecked with lips so tight you might think us just what we were—little children—and we giggled as if it was a big deal and thought that peck was the extent of romance. In a flash things changed, as they do when any of us experiences a shocking violation of this magnitude.

However, this does not change God's plans and purposes for our lives. Nor does it alter our potential impact in the world. We simply need to say to our Lord and King, "Yes, Lord, I believe!"

You see, Jesus took on the burden of all evil and sin. In the Scriptures, we learn that He was bruised for our sins and iniquities, and that "...the chastisement of our peace was upon him" (Isaiah 53:5). That means all mankind, even those who have harmed us, which is often too kind for me to understand. But I am beginning to understand, a little at a time. There truly is no final comprehension of the depth and breadth of His love for us. Just as the sun cannot exist without the moon, the stars without the sky, the earth without the sea, God has chosen to not exist without *us*, and we are His finest creation.

> **"For those whom He foreknew [of whom He was aware and loved beforehand], He also destined from the beginning [foreordaining them] to be molded into the image of His Son [and share inwardly His likeness] that He might become the firstborn among many brethren."**
>
> **Romans 8:29**

Furthermore,

> **"God said, 'Let Us [Father, Son, and Holy Spirit] make mankind in Our image, after Our likeness, and let them have complete authority over the fish of the sea, the birds of the air, the [tame] beasts, and over all of the earth, and over everything that creeps upon the earth.'"**
>
> **Genesis 1:26**

And herein lies the truth: nothing can separate us from His love, except of course, we ourselves. And that happens if we operate in the unbelief that says you are not, or I am not, as good as anyone else in creation simply because of the world's negative judgment. Or if we feel that our circumstances—like the appalling abuse I and other young girls and even boys suffered—condemned us forever. But I am here to tell you what God has said, and what He always knew: that if we believe we can overcome deep and horrible acts, we can heal from the worst of crimes and live the life that we were always ordained to live. When we rise up out of these seemingly insurmountable experiences, we have the potential not only to live anew, ourselves, but also to pull others out of the fire and ashes so that they also may live a new life. And that is a big part of what life is all about.

4

FROM THE FRYING PAN INTO THE FIRE

I POSE A QUESTION

Why is it that so-called at-risk teens that society now calls "throwaways" and we know are merely "runaways" that are raped, trafficked and victims who were attacked by a pedophile and "exposed to sexual exploitation?" But are treated like only "bad kds." This attitude is slowly but barely changing, I know; but why has it taken so long to be discussed and addressed?

I remember a time that I woke up in the parking lot of a gay club in Las Vegas, not long after I was rescued by God's grace from the brothel, with a headache that felt like my head was splitting in two. I was left for dead, the taste of drugs and alcohol on my breath and the unshowered smell on my young body. An angry guy in the bar had come up to me and knocked me out cold for no reason at all, and also knocked out my two front teeth. I began to hate my existence; again, darkness would tell me that there was nothing else to do but end my life.

I remember when The Madam "seasoned" us (that ghastly, cynical term again) of how a trafficker/pimp/predator is like a best friend, father or mother figure, big sister or brother, a pretend savior; family figure that leads their victim along in what seems like love only to cause a situation of which force fraud and coercion, positioning the victim for being trafficked. She seasoned us for her prostitution stable; I thought that I would be loved, somehow. I believed at the time that it was love, and I immediately became addicted to the drugs that were forced on me. My young mind, filled with barbiturates, heroin, strong alcohol in huge amounts, lemon 714s, and cocaine (freebasing as well as snorting it), had a false sense of hope—until it faded.

Because of these parties, which were filled with bankers, lawyers, husbands, wives, and members of the mafia, I was told—we were *all* told—that we were nothing. Besides, our pimps said (and we believed) that it was what everybody was doing. After being forced to take drugs, we became addicted, numb, and finally just didn't care.

Of course, like many young girls, I needed to believe what the pimps said. I had already been inducted and forced, and I didn't see a way out. So, for me to come to God after all of this and trust that His love was real, was difficult; and it would be throughout my life a challenge.

I remember another time, when I broke away from both The Madam and my mother's home. I was in between for a while, like many trafficked victims are now. Oftentimes, the pedophile-trafficker (pimp or madam) will let the children live at home and make them think that the relationship they have is special and secret, as though they still have freedom. Then, when it gets bad at home—and it always gets worse, especially with the pedophile planting dark, twisted thoughts and ideas—the traffickers help the children to feel that they have the freedom to choose where to live. In actual fact, the children are being controlled, seasoned, and primed for servitude or kidnapping, as I was; I do not think that there is really a difference.

My best buddy and I had 90 cents between the two of us, and we decided to run away, on Highway 15 North from Las Vegas.

The highway was hot, dry, and long, hardly a place for two young girls to be walking alone. I can still feel and hear the dry weeds crunching beneath our tennis shoes. My buddy, whom I will call Frankie to protect her privacy, carried her briefcase, a gift she had received from a family friend. We were both fairly new to having our periods. What was funny about that is that this burgundy briefcase was filled with pens, pencils, scrap paper—and tampons for the first time. It was hilarious. But you see, Frankie wanted to be a businesswoman so badly one day, and the briefcase meant the world to her.

We had both just been tainted into smoking cigarettes and were already beginning to be addicted to drugs as minors, though we had not seen the worst of it.

Kids are resilient, and we managed to laugh, joke, and even be excited about the adventure we were embarked on. It was dangerous and would turn out to be horrid, but in that moment it seemed lifesaving. We hitchhiked, treading through that desert on the dirt shoulder of the road. Tumbleweeds would blow by every now and again, and we would laugh as we whistled that old Clint Eastwood motion picture sound bite from "The Good the Bad and the Ugly."

I chuckle and cry at the same time when I think about that moment. After our thumbs were outstretched for a long time and we were getting thirsty, a car pulled up. Simultaneously, a large truck pulled in front of it, but something told us to avoid that truck and go to the car behind it.

To this day, I believe we would have been molested and murdered had we taken the truck or that something worse than sudden death would have happened. I had heard of a girl who had been raped and had gotten her arms cut off in that desert. We had no business being there. The car we did get into was like stepping way back in time to the 1950s, an old blue Buick driven by an elderly White couple. As we settled into the car, it seemed like a fairy tale to us.

It was clean, with beautiful upholstery, and it smelled like something sweet. The woman had her hair pulled back and wore a button-down sweater; the man wore a plaid shirt. Their clothes didn't look real, you see, they seemed too perfect and the way in which they spoke to us was like something out of a film or novel. It didn't seem earthly. Well, the unique quality of the sound itself, when I listened to them speak, was and is powerful, even now, in my memory. It was like something I had never heard before. They sounded tender and untrue; too kind to be real as I had never met anyone as caring from start to finish. They also spoke with a different rhythm that I can't explain and their English was very proper as well.

"The speed of sound is the distance travelled during a unit of time by a sound wave propagating through an elastic medium. In dry air (68 °F or 20 °C) the speed of sound is 343.2 meters per second (1,126 ft/s). This is 1,236 kilometers per hour (768 mph), or about one kilometer in three seconds or approximately one mile in five seconds."[1]

Remember what I said earlier about sound waves, which is sound in general. Well, the couple's speech sounded different—heavenly—and I felt safe in their presence. In Genesis we read, "they heard the sound of the Lord God walking in the garden in the cool of the day" (Genesis 3:8). But since God didn't walk with feet, then what was that sound? This is so powerful to ponder: the fact that when God speaks and/or moves,

His sound has a certain quality, a certain peace and an ineffable reality.

But what about the speed of light, how is it a part of this? You see, in God's sound and in His words of love dwell His light,

> **"...the illuminating light of the Gospel of the glory of Christ (the Messiah)."**
>
> **2 Corinthians 4:4**

And,

"…in Your light, do we see light."

Psalms 36:9

The speed of light and sound are factual scientific measures, but if you add that to what we don't understand, it gives us a beautiful depiction of the power of loving and encouraging words, God's presence, which then suffuses our thoughts and our words. This is what I felt with the blessed angels in human form who picked up Frankie and me. Here is what science says about the speed of light:

"Light is exactly 299,792,458 metres per second, a figure that is exact because the length of the metre is defined from this constant and the international standard for time. In imperial units this speed is approximately 186,282 miles per second."[2]

One hundred eighty-six thousand-plus miles per second! Amazing power! As the Bible says, they ascend and descend (John1:51).

ANGELS ARE REAL, AND THEY ARE IN GOD'S ARMY

Being in the car felt so surreal that Frankie and I chuckled, like kids do, and with eyes slanted, stared at one another like, "What?!" The woman said, "So, where are you young ladies headed?" Frankie and I quickly responded, "Los Angeles."

The man, who was driving calmly and steadily, said, "I've hitchhiked before, a long time ago. You all need to be careful out here." "Yes, sir," we replied. We all sat in silence for a bit, and the lady said, "Well, we are going as far as Barstow." After that, Frankie drifted off to sleep. I was staring out of the window, just wondering what life would bring, and in that moment I was comfortable. I was very glad to be in that car; there was such an amazing peace there, and it is even tangible to me now, as I recall it.

I drifted off to sleep.

A while later, we were awakened by the sudden, startling sound of gravel crunching under the tires, and the car came to a complete stop.

They turned around to face us, our eyes met, and I could hear that vinyl-seat-cover sound squeaking as their bodies twisted to get a good look at us. It sounded like music to my ears as they kindly told us, "Take care of yourselves." The music faded. I didn't want to leave, because I felt love in that car. But I knew we had to, so we got out and watched them drive away.

We stood there, frozen and quiet, as the remaining dust from the gravel that the tires kicked up subsided all around us. I felt like crying, but I didn't want Frankie to feel worse. I believe with all of my heart that they were bona fide angels. This is one of two times in my life that I have known this.

The Bible says:

> **"Be not forgetful to entertain strangers: for thereby some have entertained angels unawares."**
>
> **Hebrews 13:2 (KJV)**

*

"If we were to look at our brain, we may see a dark abscess caused by the stronghold of anger. The same is true for envy, anxiety, lust, fear, depression, and other emotions."[8]

Kimberly Davidson,
Author, "Breaking the Cover Girl Mask"

I was at the age, as a minor, where the subconscious mind begins to hold onto things with vivid recall, on even deeper levels. And after that moment through the desert, things got worse. My mind held onto painful experiences and, for the first time, with all that I had already been through, I started to see my life as one that would have to scratch its way to survival. After we were dropped off by The Angels, we were near an exit. We could see beyond us only one restaurant. It was late, so we headed toward it—Sambo's Restaurant, I think, was its name, off the interstate. It was cold and windy—the desert at night in the wintertime, ugh. We spent the night in an engine room after *borrowing* five dollars from an unlocked diesel truck that was parked in a lot full of them for food. Inside the restaurant, we ordered a plate of French fries with so much ketchup on them that the waitress could tell we were in trouble.

Two young Black girls and all White patrons in this little diner was already strange enough, but the ongoing requests for ketchup and crackers didn't help. The girls in the brothel were Black, Asian, and White at the time. To this day, I know that color has nothing to do with God, but it is something that mankind has allowed to divide us from ourselves and one another. So when the waitress brought the free Saltine crackers that we requested, and sneered, I locked eyes with her and smiled. Her heart seemed to soften, and she broke down and gave us a bunch more. "It's amazing what a simple smile can do," I thought, especially one that was so obviously screaming for mercy. It seemed that she realized we were kids and something was wrong. Unfortunately, like most folks, she probably thought, who wants to get involved with a couple of *runaways*?

We found a way to survive another day. Frankie filled her briefcase with sugar packets and a few crackers. We paid the check and searched around in the dark until we found a place to sleep. The engine room in the back of the restaurant would be that spot. It had a very noisy water heater, but at least it was warmer than the outside.

We lay on the cold cement and squeezed each other tightly to stay warm. I remember listening to the noise, hearing cars passing by on the interstate and diesel trucks coming and going. It was a huge diesel truck stop; truckers had filled the diner earlier.

I found myself restless, scared; but the sound of crickets calmed me that night. They still have that effect on me today. But I still couldn't sleep because my mind wandered throughout the night.

I wondered what would become of us. Frankie knew I could not sleep, so she placed her hand on my side and started to rock me to sleep. I guess it worked, eventually, at least for a few hours, and it became a ritual that I did not break until many years later. I would rock myself to sleep, without Frankie of course, but I rocked.

The next morning, we woke up smack dab in the middle of a huge puddle of water. "Dang it, I can't stand this, I can't stand this," she screamed. I tried to comfort her by making jokes, which is what she did for me when I was often extremely troubled. Our clothes were soaked, but we had to hit the road—wet, cold, and hungry again. I knew a schoolteacher who had left our school in Vegas and moved to California, so we hitchhiked there in hopes he would help. The last time he helped me, he forced me to have rape sex with him; by this time in my life, it seemed that was the norm. It seemed that most of the men we had met so far had taken innocence from me, and that that was all that was on their minds. Even the married ones with families were not faithful. We assumed that this was normal. I am not sure if it was because of the pimp and Madam and how we had to live, but there were so very many men who were pedophiles. The sad thing is, I don't know if they understood that pedophilia is a deeply pathological perversion, and they may never understand, especially if they are never confronted or prosecuted for it.

The terms *pedophilia* or *pedophile* have a range of definitions found in common usage, psychology, and law enforcement. As a medical diagnosis, pedophilia is defined as a psychological disorder in which an adult experiences a sexual preference for minor children. Pedophilia is a form of paraphilia, or abnormal form of arousal, in which a person either has acted on intense sexual urges toward minor children or has sexual urges toward and fantasies about minor children that cause the individual distress or interpersonal difficulty.[4]

THERE IS NO SUCH THING AS A YOUNG GIRL WITH AN OLDER MAN, IT IS ALWAYS A PEDOPHILE WITH A VICTIM.

If we are too afraid to call it what it is and talk about, much less confront, the molestation, rape, and incest that has occurred in our own families, our churches, and in a myriad of other settings, how will these predators ever know that what they do is deeply wrong and horribly destructive to their victims? How will they know we will not tolerate this evil any longer? And how can they ever have the insight, the self-revelation that they are in fact predators?

These crimes are root causes of and precursors to someone's being trafficked in the first place and whether street, brothel, motel, online, or familial sex-slavery, it's all the same. Moreover, when will law enforcement begin to stop pushing rape cases out the door? When victims come in, as mentioned, a high percentage are ignorantly dismissed because of victims coming in drunk and not of legal drinking age, or in stress the victim has a hard time being confronted my a male officer she freezes up or is angry or other issues such as "lack of evidence"; but in these cases, evidence can be subjective. A traumatized, confused girl often screams the facts of the rape or woman who is suffering from symptoms that police officers are not equipped to understand. Or someone the victim knows, as with familial trafficking, which creates fear and confusion in her heart and mind, committed the rape-crime. The police and authorities sometimes look down on the traumatized victim with impatient contempt, and she is summarily dismissed. The idea that one in five girls on college campuses in the

U.S.A. will be raped is frightening.

This creates a noxiously beneficial environment for the trafficker, who thinks, "Well, only a few rape cases ever go to trial and hardly any get convictions so , forget about age 18. I'm going down the rabbit hole to using girls 17, 16, 15, 14, 13, 12, 11, 10, 9, 8, 7,….and why not age 6, 5, 4, 3, 2, 1." As I mentioned, one of the most horrific cases I learned of was a six-month-old infant who was used for sex by a pedophile.

The trafficker (pimp, trick, madam, john, and all pedophiles) knows his/her odds of getting away with it are decent. So, it's safer to sell babies instead of guns or drugs or anything else, for that matter? They don't even have to put the kids on the corner. They just post pictures or video online and call it an escort service, or pornography, or dates with other consenting adults when the victims are really children of all ages and women who are broken and lost down the rabbit hole.

The fact is, these criminals are actually and unfortunately getting away with murder and nothing less. As I said in common usage, the term pedophile refers to an adult who is sexually attracted to minor children, whether or not the adult acts upon that attraction by sexually abusing a minor child.

I think the previous definition clarifies any misconceptions of what a pedophile is. What we also need to understand is why good, mature, moral men are so important to the health of our society, and so badly needed. In these dark times, confused and distorted values in our society have obscured that importance. In our troubled society, people allow themselves to be driven by their fleshly desires, with no honest heart and no real love, because true love will pay the price of its innate high calling.

Waiting until marriage, or chastity, has not been historically successful. I know this is unpopular but, truth be told, what is wrong with waiting? There is a real beauty in getting to know someone slowly and finally coming in trust to sexual union, which is a beautiful benefit of a healthy marriage.

It is beyond reason why fornication has been the age-old follow-the-leader death trap that countless millions of men and women have fallen into over and over, and over and over again. Even King Solomon said:

> **"Then I looked on all that my hands had done and the labor I had spent in doing it, and behold, all was vanity and a striving after the wind *and* a feeding on it, and there was no profit under the sun."**
>
> **Ecclesiastes 2:11**

Furthermore, we find that out of all he possessed, Solomon realized that it was God that mattered, and that being content in what he had was key. "Under the sun" in the above Scripture reminds me of what is above it: God Himself is my portion. I learned later that "to lose my life for His sake," I would eventually find it. This by no means is saying that we should not obtain romance and wealth, but only so long as our material goods and our flesh don't own and rule us.

My revelation about this, which is expressed in most faiths, including mine, is born out of great pain and the many rape and foul sex acts that I have endured and witnessed.

At that point in my young life, when Frankie and I ran away to Los Angeles, all I cared about was finding warm and loving shelter, food, clothing—basic human needs. What I longed for most and what I really hoped my schoolteacher would provide for us was love. I hoped that he would save us, not realizing that pedophiles can't do that, nor do they want to. They are driven by their sick desires.

Traffickers and pimps season/condition victims for prostitution by raping them and yet, mixing in, a little affection. They fill the young heads with thoughts of how they want to be loved, making them believe the abusers are the only ones who can supply what they need in life.

And this, mind you, is often spoken of while the victims are getting beaten "upside the head." Understand: it is common for the trafficker to let his friends rape their merchandise. And then to tell the victims all the things they did wrong in order for this to be happening to them.

I was so young in heart and mind that I began to believe them. I thought that something was wrong with me when I was raped and abused, that I brought it on myself. After all, my father had left us, and most kids who think their own father doesn't love them will think something must be wrong with themselves. I was no different. Unfortunately, children suffer in divorce when the parents are not able to communicate and have a strong disdain toward each other.

They allowed me to go home, as I have mentioned. When things got bad or challenging at home, as they do for many teens, especially those in seriously dysfunctional families, the pimps pretended to come in and save the day and give their prey an escape route. But they were, in fact, a huge part of the problem and oftentimes they create the problems. This is one of the reasons that so many females in our society—a huge number of them age 17 and under—do not tell that they have been raped. What I didn't know, and many children and young people don't fully comprehend, was that the pedophile/trafficker had already robbed us of our innocence and self-respect it will take years to find again, if we do at all.

For the males I met who were raped or sexually violated by men when they were kids or as children, it is an even lonelier road. Many never find their true manhood after abuse because not enough men ever dare admit and share/discuss their trauma with others. With God all things are possible, but what if they do not hear of God?

What if victims don't know how wonderful He truly is and that He (God Almighty) is not the reason for the vile and wicked things that have taken place?

I tell you, had it not been for those who reached out to me here and there and had the gall, nerve, boldness, and gentle love to tell me about the goodness of God, I have no idea where I would be now. I must say, some of the kindest people were not officially "believers." Some believers would later judge me and, in a religious spirit, cause me to second-guess the Lord's love for me.

But other truly compassionate and generous people one could call believers cared for me, just as I was, even if I chose not to seek Him out just then for fear I would get my heart broken again. They showed me love all the more. The Word of God states:

> **"Beware of false prophets, who come to you dressed as sheep, but inside they are devouring wolves. You will fully recognize them by their fruits. Do people pick grapes from thorns, or figs from thistles?"**
>
> **Matthew 7:15-20**

It was through BOTH non-believers and certain believers who loved me as I was and told me that God did too—that I eventually would long to know Him again as I did when I was a small child all on my own. I want to tell you later how I was born from above, so excuse this sidebar. I do realize it was those who *called* themselves Christians who were Nazis who imprisoned Jews during the Holocaust. Others that called themselves Christians also kidnapped Africans, raping and killing them by the millions (millions upon millions of Africans were murdered) through the Middle Passage and Slavery. Once these particular traffickers because that is what they were when they forced other human beings into slavery, reached America and other parts of the world, they even killed and tortured Black slaves for sport. Slavery is not new, and modern day slavery or human trafficking is another form of it that preys on others and violates human rights in shocking, violent ways. In addition, the Lord has shown me that many in the world are in bondage of some sort and are being trafficked in some way by the evil one. Some people move to and through life by the enemy's guidance and prodding and not by the *staff* of God, nor by the Holy Spirit.

Trafficking is a form of bondage and exploitation, and people are often exploited in various ways. In the realm of darkness, there are set-ups, devices, and smokescreens where many often live their lives as though life was only for them, just as I once did. The gender-based violence (GBV) in the world and evil acts against children are a sign of the times, revealing very deep and profound wounds and ills in society and in societal thinking.

Many don't always see it, especially here in America. Through prayer and revelation, science, evaluation, coming together from all walks of life, and with God's help, we can confront these monstrosities. We cannot simply put a Band-Aid on the symptoms, but with God's strength and truth we can go right for the root causes.

The selfish life only seems like a happy life from the outside, but there is nothing more powerful than laying one's life down and then finding it reborn as it is and was meant to be in God!

> **"No one has greater love [no one has shown stronger affection] than to lay down (give up) his own life for his friends."**
>
> **John 15:13**

Scriptures also say:

> **"...he who loses his life for My sake will find it!"**
>
> **Matthew 16:25**

I often speak in churches, community centers, government agencies, nonprofit and for-profit organizations, and it has taken me a long time to share such things. I was so very afraid of what others would think and that I would be looked at as foul. People might wonder how my husband, or any man would want to marry someone like me. Could I ever feel clean, with all of these eyes looking down on me? But Jesus paid the full price to do just that! To redeem me in every way and on every level, just as He does for all of us, regardless of what has taken place. He washed it all away in His precious blood that was shed on Calvary. But how could I fully receive it? I couldn't pretend anymore that I was okay. I honestly think people knew I wasn't happy but thought that it was probably that I was just "different." I had to escape the prison that I was placed in by those who abused me. I could no longer be the one who was blocking my own release.

Scriptures powerfully say:

> **"Let the redeemed of the Lord say so, whom He has delivered from the hand of the adversary, And gathered them out of the lands, from the east and from the west, from the north and from the [Red] Sea in the south. Then they cried to the Lord in their trouble, and He saved them out of their distresses. He brought them out of darkness and the shadow of death and broke apart the bonds that held them."**
>
> **Psalms 107:3-4, 13-14**

When I heard the message of Christ, I understood more of who I was. I also realized I needed additional help, because I could not fully trust God and needed practical steps, for which cognitive therapy helped. Believe it or not, it is similar to speaking the Word repeatedly over you. Powerful, right? This is why I worked with therapists who were believers or at least knew that I was and respected it in every way, as does any great doctor or teacher.

Not everyone who names the name of Christ is a real lover of God; this is evident throughout history. We all fall short often, and the exciting news is that God still loves us all. Later, I longed to have the fruit, which showed I did have that love. After seeing so much ugliness, I longed to see love in action. The Bible says this:

> **"[What, what would have become of me] had I not believed that I would see the Lord's goodness in the land of the living!"**
>
> **Psalms 27:13**

I realized that believers and non-believers who were searching for God reminded me of the uncircumcised man, about whom the Lord spoke,

> **"So if a man who is uncircumcised keeps the requirements of the Law, will not his uncircumcision be credited to him as [equivalent to] circumcision? Then those who are physically uncircumcised but keep the Law will condemn you who, although you have the code in writing and have circumcision, break the Law. For he is not a [real] Jew who is only one outwardly *and* publicly, nor is [true] circumcision something external and physical. But he is a Jew who is one inwardly, and [true] circumcision is of the heart, a spiritual and not a literal [matter]. His praise is not from men but from God."**
>
> **2 Romans 2:25-29**

Thank the Lord God that He sees in us things we rarely see in ourselves until He takes the time to show us! This, of course, has been the huge war in my own mind. I am certain that many go through the same thing for one reason or another. Most victims who grow to be survivors who thrive through hard work don't always understand their value, and that is when God cleanses us through His divine love and Grace; it is definite and sure.

The blood of Jesus cleanses us of all unrighteousness, even that which was not caused by our own doing and has become a part of how we see ourselves, our own lives, our environment, and those around us.

For whatever reason and at any time, the Lord is ready to take us all in, because in Him we are no longer alone, orphaned, or unworthy. That is what Paul means when he says

> **"for *My* strength *and* power are made perfect (fulfilled and completed) *and show themselves most effective* in [your] weakness."**
>
> **2 Corinthians 12:9**

He also makes us virginal again and the slate is wiped clean, without blemish or stain in HIM! This was absolutely important for me. How could I think of marrying and having the right to achieve dreams? How could I make love to my husband with hang-ups, uneasiness, or weirdness? Let's be real! If, in fact, the marriage bed is supposed to be undefiled, according to the Word of God, was I going to defile it by bringing my past into it? Was my husband going to judge me in arguments? Was he going to think his acts of fornication were cleaner, or made him cleaner than me?

Or was I going to think that I did not deserve happiness in marriage? Thank God my husband always tells me what a wonderful wife I am. But more importantly, God tells me always that I am His beautiful bride! I think that is why my husband and I waited until our wedding night to know each other, to fully consummate our union and commitment to each other. And how God has blessed us!

Of course, we don't want to bring our past into our future, but most people bring their baggage into the bedroom when married because we have not cleaned house, broken soul ties, and just simply let go of old emotional baggage. Yet, how can we let go of that heavy baggage when we are suffering from profound trauma and have stopped growing at the "point of impact"(as I like to call it) of that trauma?

I was a woman-child. I looked all grown up, but was in many ways stuck at the age where the trauma of abuse first impacted me. Besides prayer, deliverance, and worship, we also need wisdom and good counsel. We often may need to try various types of therapy with a bona fide psychologist who understands our spiritual aspirations. And we need to learn to trust God and walk in holiness before Him, to discover who we really are and what our purpose is, in Him. I needed that then and still do! I needed to understand practical things, for instance, how what I ate, what I didn't eat, hormones, neurotransmitters, exercise, my thought life, my prayer life, my environment—how all these elements affect the discovery of my true identity and my purpose, long forgotten.

This identity and life purpose for many victims of child abuse is not always fully discovered, but I believe it can be. I needed to know all of this and somehow thought in running away I would find what I did not even know I was looking for all the time. And that was God the Father and the treasures that are found only in Him.

Frankie and I finally made it to Los Angeles after we ran away. I found the teacher I had known and whom I had hoped would help us. He stood at the door of his home and allowed us in for a few minutes; but then told us he could not do any more for us, gave us a little money for a motel and a few days' food, and told us to leave. Because we had sexual relations, I had thought he would have feelings for me, and would have some idea of helping me and my friend—some idea of how we could live. I was too young and naïve to know that the rape of a young girl by pedophiles who sometimes disguise themselves as boyfriends is evil and was never love. Even adult women need to understand this on a profound level. I told Frankie that surely he would help us, but he didn't!

We had already gone down a short list of people we might be able to reach.. She had an aunt somewhere, and I had a grandmother, but they were both in New York City. I had never met my grandmother, but I thought she might be alive and that she lived in Queens. One moment I was standing in the living room of someone whom I thought loved me, and the next moment, I was back out on the street, with no idea where my friend and I would go next. I thought because he didn't beat me that it must have been love, but what does a broken child know of love, never having experienced it. The odd thing is that he had a girlfriend who would come with him to see me but I realized only later that she didn't know he was raping me. I thought it was a relationship, and is girlfriend thought he was this cool teacher helping a youth in need.

Part 2

Discovery Is a Process

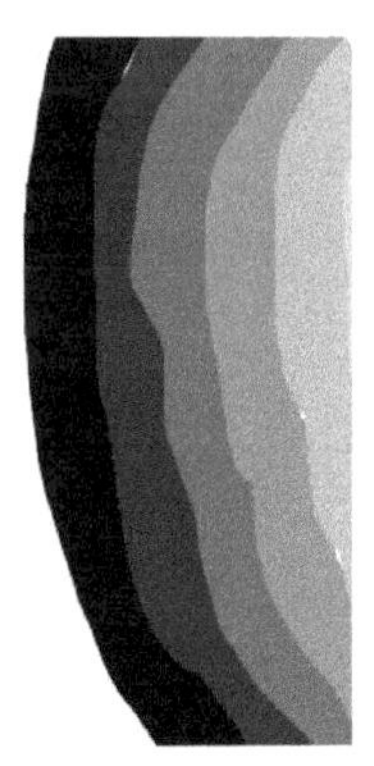

5

REACH

"Children, I talks to God and God talks to me.
I goes out and talks to God in de fields and de woods.
Dis morning I was walking out, and I got over de fence.
I saw de wheat a holding up its head, looking very big.
I goes up and takes holt ob it. You b'lieve it, dere was no
wheat dare? I says, God, what is de matter wid dis wheat?
And he says to me, 'Sojourner, dere is a little weasel in it.'
Now I hears talkin' about de Constitution and de rights of
man. I comes up and I takes hold of dis Constitution.
It looks mighty big, and I feels for my rights,
but der aint any dare. Den I says, God, what ails dis
Constitution? He says to me,
'Sojourner, dere is a little weasel in it.'"

Sojourner Truth
Author, Abolitionist, Activist, Former Slave

I hadn't thought much about any rights I might have had as a human being; and since I had not been saved yet, I surely hadn't thought of what living in the righteousness of God meant.

Isn't it something that, even now, many of us do not know of or are not acquainted with our rights? We do not comprehend that slavery in all forms is wrong, including that which we suffer through rape and sexual bondage. Through the sacrificial blood of Jesus, we are no longer enslaved to anything or anyone. We are to be free thinkers, living a life of victory.

Later on in life, I wondered about this. But before I tell you a bit later how I came to Christ, I long to share something I experienced afterward, and involves when Jesus talks about the "Leaven of the Pharisees and Sadducees:"

> **"Jesus said to them, Be careful *and* on your guard against the leaven (ferment) of the Pharisees and Sadducees. And they reasoned among themselves about it, saying, *It is* because we did not bring any bread. But Jesus, aware of this, asked, Why are you discussing among yourselves the fact that you have no bread? O you [men, how little trust you have in Me, how] little faith!"**
>
> **Matthew 16:6-8**

Eventually, I would find my way to a God who loved me, who loves us all incomparably and with an understanding unfathomable to humans. A God who knew me, who had always known me.

It was this God, this Lord, who would in His divine love be able to share with me what my life was truly meant for and how to go about reaching for it and walking in that destiny. It would be in the future that I would one day also discover that it is through relationships that we grow and learn, that we reach beyond our own shallow capacity that only grows in the unity of God's love.

But we also have to be careful of the leaven, which is what many of us don't face and need to get rid of in our own lives. Mine was thinking that I was meant to be a doormat and that I could never be pure again and that abuse is common and that there is no way to change it. This is a leaven that I've worked on for a long time. There is no relationship that can be true and yet one-sided. God, in all of His glory, is the master of relationships. God the Father created all things by His Word and without Him was not anything made (John 1: 1-4). Jesus, when He knew what was to happen during His crucifixion, burial, and resurrection, said that the Father would not leave us comfortless, but send in His name the Holy Spirit, who would teach us all things (John 14:26). This is such a beautiful depiction of our relationship with God, by the Holy Spirit. As odd as it sounds, He allows us to show *Him* things because of the reciprocity found in a loving relationship. These things are what are called natural, and *natural* in Greek means "God-given."

It is amazing that God would even allow Himself to be pleasantly surprised by us, to have exceeding joy when we follow Him and follow through.

This is one of limitless beauties, which declare God's magnificence. He is all-knowing and yet chooses us, but He also requires that we still have to choose Him; and He waits until our very last breath if He must. In the Book of Isaiah, He declares to the children of Israel that there is no other God but Him, and with passion He asks them to come back, to return unto Him. How gorgeous is that?

The Bible says we are Abraham's seed and joint heirs of the promise, and that there is now in the Body of Christ neither Jew nor Greek, neither bond nor free (Galatians 3:28). He declares that there is no other God besides him, and that He is the only One that loves us so (Isaiah 45).

I would later say things like, "I can make it!" Some would scream, "You can make it if you try!" I would discover this after I eventually escaped the hand of a trafficker in a Los Angeles apartment after being picked up by him from Sunset Boulevard and bent over his balcony; a man with a razor blade, threatening to slice up my face. My young body walked the streets in the slavery that some call *forced prostitution.* Can you imagine my little body out there on the streets, wondering if this would be my life forever and if the first man that purchased me would be the one to save me? This is where I ended up after my encounter with the schoolteacher and before Frankie and I escaped to New York City. Can you imagine how dirty, filthy, and unclean I must have felt? Unfortunately, this violence and discrimination exists toward abused and trafficked children, which delays or entirely prevents healing.

It is the same discrimination of thinking such things as "oh that happens in third world countries," or "those are those kind of girls or boys that get caught up in craziness" that kind of bigotry breeds the victimization of others and was the root cause of slavery, which has always been wrong.

Frankie and I had met the man who bent me over the balcony in the Los Angeles apartment with a woman he said was his sister, two strangers who offered to take us for what we thought was just a meal, a little food to take the edge off our hunger. We had shared only a hot dog, drowned in ketchup and relish, in the last 24 hours.

This was right after we had gotten to Los Angeles. They seemed nice at first, and invited us back to their place to get some clean clothes and maybe to "crash" a night at their place, which seemed a lot better than the engine room of a truck stop.

After we had left the schoolteacher, we had camped on the floor of a large apartment with a group of gypsies and a couple of other outcasts who took us in for whatever they needed. I was raped on the roof that night. Thing is, I was a good kid, a once great student, even though horrible things happened after my earlier rape. But with my issues in rural California and our family's move to Las Vegas, things changed. Even more. For the worse. Once I met Frankie, I was already running away one to three days at a time, and even with all of that abuse and trafficking, I still was resilient, as kids are. I did not realize the damage I was suffering through it all, just as the young girls I work with today do not. Our revelations about how those violent experiences affect our soul often happens much later.

That early evening, Frankie and I were sitting along the brick wall off Sunset Boulevard, where women walked around being prostituted, many looking like death in human disguise. The man and his "sister" drove up at a time when we were more than desperate. They had nice big smiles and asked if we were hungry, saying they had been where we were and liked to help girls like us. They must have been in their early to mid thirties. We got in the car and went along *believing* what the lady said. We believed that she really had some clothing she could give us and that they liked to help youth in trouble because they had once been in trouble as well and someone helped them. It was a great line—and deadly. We came to learn that this woman was really his "bottom girl" (a prostitute or sex slave who helps a pimp "recruit" other girls), and not at all, his sister.

That day on Sunset Boulevard and all the ugly things that followed caused me to lose all hope, as it was ugly; the evil behind closed doors is sick, but what I thought was bad became worse.

I would learn that it was God, my present Redeemer and Deliverer who, at the moment He knelt in the Garden of Gethsemane, was preparing to save my soul for what I would go through. In that hour, He knew that God the Father had to let Him carry the cross for us. In that moment, God the Father could not look on Him in the same manner, for He carried all of our sins and iniquity. It was then that Jesus the Christ, the Son of the Living God, said,

> **"My Father, if it is possible, let this cup pass away from Me; nevertheless, not what I will [not what I desire], but as You will *and* desire."**
>
> **Matthew 26:39**

He did it and He made it for us. We only need to love him! He carried all of our guilt because His love is great for the Father and great for us. He carried all the shame, confusion, dysfunction, bad upbringings, lack of true riches, sickness, depression, and demonic oppression. It was the Father's will that this be done and the vile evil of man be placed on the shoulders of His Son. So much so, that the Lord would say before he took up the ghost, "It is finished!" Thus, I believe this remains true:

> **"If the Son therefore shall make you free, ye shall be free indeed!"**
>
> **John 8:36 (KJV)**

In that moment, Jesus was operating fully as God's beloved Son and our everlasting Redeemer. All we need to do is take the first step and reach! Don't look back. Take now the hand of the loving Savior, Elohim, Yahweh. Reach in, and by the Holy Spirit, you should keep reaching and leaning whenever and how much you need to. I did!

> **"For God is not a man that He should lie, nor the son of man that He should repent, has He not spoken and will not do it and has He not said it and will not make it good?"**
>
> **Numbers 23:19 (KJV)**

God is honestly neither male nor female.

> **"God is a Spirit (a spiritual Being) and those who worship Him must worship *Him* in spirit and in truth (reality)."**
>
> **John 4:24**

He likens Himself as Father because of the order of things, and that is a beautiful concept. Yet it is not as we see things, for

"His ways are higher than our Ways."

Isaiah 55:8

All we need do is take the hand, His hand. We may feel like we are walking in the dark, and maybe at times we will be, but not when we are holding the hand of the One who knows exactly who we are and where we need to go. Even with all I went through, people ask, "when did you get out of trafficking?" While many of us who experience it – come to understand that we were in and out physically because we were not out mentally, thus it is complicated to describe the bondage of going back to the filth that enslaves you in brokenness. But think of it, isn't that what happens when Christians fornicate, or lie, or get caught up in sin?

So, we all need to reach for the hand of God, which is already reaching out for you, for me, for us. Amen, Hallelujah!

6

THE MIND IS THE BATTLEFIELD

In the unique balance of God's Amazing Grace, His omniscience, His divine plans and purposes, we have a right to choose: life or death. Amazing.

We have a choice to walk through the narrow gate, which leads to life, or the broad one, which leads to death. How can this be? Does foreknowledge mean predestination?

Or can we change our future even though the outcome is known, and still surprise God with our decisions to follow His ways? I think it is all of the above. His ways, according to Scriptures, are "higher" than our ways. There are mysteries to life and ways to God that we as human beings cannot fathom; this is the astounding "sovereignty" of God. We cannot comprehend fully the profound depths of God and creation until much later in our development, but He can do what He wills. I think if we tried, at least for me, our brains would explode.

> **"But now faith is the substance of things hoped for and the evidence of things not seen."**
>
> **Hebrews 11:1 (KJV)**

And this is the faith that I fight to walk in every day.

> **For now we are looking in a mirror that gives only a dim (blurred) reflection [of reality as in a riddle or enigma], but then [when perfection comes] we shall see in reality *and* face to face! Now I know in part (imperfectly), but then I shall know *and* understand fully *and* clearly, even in the same manner as I have been fully *and* clearly known *and* understood [by God]."**
>
> **1 Corinthians 13:12**

Some things will be revealed to us, and others, we will not know—but the point is, do we trust God? Or will we *learn* to trust Him?

I eventually chose life, but it was not easy after what I had experienced. My life may not have always been easy, but, nevertheless, it's my life, my challenges to rise above and my mental soundness and good character was fought for in the realm of the supernatural. Not so sure about that? I wanted to know God, and my time would eventually come. When it did, I would see that not only could He remove the pain and sickness of my past from the center of my heart, but I wouldn't even reek of it! Allow me...

> **"And the satraps, the deputies, the governors, and the king's counselors gathered around together and saw these men—that the fire had no power upon their bodies, nor was the hair of their head singed; neither were their garments scorched *or* changed in color *or* condition, nor had even the smell of smoke clung to them."**
>
> **Daniel 3:27**

I love the fact that the smell of that evil deed, the smoke, had not even *clung* to them. Are you kidding me?! You mean that after that supernatural experience in the fiery furnace—which is what my past felt like and perhaps yours too, or that of someone you know—you mean to say that even the clothing of Hananiah, Mishael, and Azariah did not reek of the past, did not even smell like smoke?

You may or may not recognize those names; they are the actual birth names of the three men who triumphantly survived that furnace unscathed. It was the unbelieving king who served other gods who gave them other names: Shadrach, Meshach, and Abednego. He tried to change their destiny by changing their names, because in that era, the changing of a name was part of altering a person's destiny. That is why God changed the names of so many in the Scriptures.

Even after the drama of the three faithful men emerging from the furnace untouched, the king still broke a false promise he had given them. Even after all God had done for him, through the Hebrew boys and Daniel, the king's allegiance was still not to them or their God but to himself! But look at this, even in all of that betrayal and seemingly near-death experiences, God used these trials to build their strength and their faith, and ours, all of these centuries later.

Many traffickers change the names of their victims. In the brothel they give you names like Candy and Sweet Julie or any name that is not your birth name.

Some are names that are curse words or phrases like "the king's dog" or worse. So the traffickers—the pimps and madams gave us made-up, cheap, demeaning names by which we were known to their customers. And even out in the professional world of social workers, health professionals, academics, and the law, they call you "at risk," "teenage prostitute," and many names that are not your birth name. It cuts both ways, it seems—and we are the ones being cut. But none of this is true in God's eyes—and remains so only if we believe it. I referred to the Biblical men as having a near-death experience, because they could have died; yet they chose to believe God.

For instance, Daniel, could have been eaten by the lion, but he chose to believe God. Many, such as King David, chose to take God at His word by dealing with challenges in a supernatural way, which was on his knees, our knees, in prayer, in fasting, in spending time with the Lord. God loves spending time with you. He is jealous for you! I would learn much later how much God loved me, but my first step was simply believing. I could no longer cry about yesterday, even though it hurt. I had to break through.

Being too religious is an understatement, for being a narrowly religious Pharisee caused them to think Christ was evil, more than 2,000 years ago. It is the very thing that crucified our Lord afresh, according to the Scriptures.

It is important for me to share how I came to know Jesus, my very best Friend, my Master, and my Salvation.

Oh, what a friend we have in Jesus! Oh, glory, I feel the Holy Spirit blasting me right now! Whom shall I fear and of whom shall I be afraid, for Thou art with me! Amen.

Prayer Corner

Thank you Lord, for your goodness. Thank you Lord, for all you do for us, for each and every person reading this book right now, God! Thank you for touching them right where they are! I decree and declare supernatural healing and the presence of your awesome love to cover them like they have never known or experienced before, even if for the first time, Lord God!!! Thank you, Holy Spirit, for showing them who you are and shining the light of the glorious Gospel and the Living God right in their midst!!! Lord, remove EVERY hindrance from their path, so they discover the one that leads to you and ALL you have and have always had for them.

Bless you, God. Amen!

"Those are the same stars, and that is the same moon,
that look down upon your brothers and sisters,
and which they see as they look up to them, though
they are ever so far away from us, and each other."

Sojourner Truth
Author, Abolitionist, Activist, Former Slave

"God is no respecter of persons" (Acts 10:34, KJV) according to the Word of God, so if He was going to make me clean, then surely I was going to let Him give it a go!

I left the brothel—and with many survivors there is not always just one because each motel room, house, and apartment turns into one. Nor is there ever just one pimp; there is the one that turned you out; which is the first person that introduces you or seasons you thereby stealing your mind into darkness or turning you out, which could have been someone you think is a boyfriend but was a pimp all along; or an older, best girlfriend, who turns you out and is really a bottom girl, recruiting; or a teacher who pretends to love you; or even a trick who takes you to a "friend." They are all adults, and it is rape, and they all fit the bill of a trafficker. Fact remains, I was lost. After many painful experiences, I had found my way in a few states and ended up back in Las Vegas, only to decide to move back to Los Angeles, where I had lived as a small child, to try and start something new. The final escort service that I was in, which was associated with a house (brothel), got in huge trouble. Later on the madam, who held things together for the pimp/trafficker became sick and the fact that I eventually escaped from Los Angles in the first place was incredible but then I was back and forth with traffickers until I understood on some level the bondage that I was in. The police busted the place in Las Vegas and it was in all of that that Frankie and I were able to leave unnoticed. Eventually, even though back and forth, and suffering, I was out of the trafficking but still addicted to drugs. When I began to learn that I might have a choice, the beginnings of understanding the work I had to do to be free started.

Once I made it back to Los Angles, I took a job at a local restaurant near Beverly Hills that was frequented by all of the Hollywood folk. I loved that because they all seemed as crazy as I felt; it helped me avoid the temptation of blowing my brains out, because profound thoughts of suicide crippled me often.

The devil, which I then thought was myself talking, would whisper insidious things in my mind, such as:

"Don't you know you're ugly? Don't you realize that you're gross and unclean? Can't you see that there is no real reason for you to be here? You're in agony, and no one is going to really ever love you."

"Your mother doesn't love you; your father doesn't love you; he didn't even raise you! Don't you realize, Brook, that it's really too late for you?"

"You have nothing, your thoughts are all over the place, and you can't focus; you're crazy. Don't you know that? You're not in your right mind and you will never be." "Dreams, you can forget about those, too, because with the fear that has you scared to sleep in the dark or even stand in front of anyone, there is no way you will ever be free or fulfill any dream."

"SO GIVE UP, DO IT NOW, END YOUR LIFE!"

This was endless for awhile. I was gripped by depression and anxiety. I was very uncomfortable in my own skin, still fighting all types of addictions, such as being addicted not only to drugs but to hyper chaos and disorder; all I wanted was just the feeling of being high, of escaping my dark thoughts. And, at that time, I thought I was homosexual, gay, or lesbian.

I didn't know what to do and was afraid to do anything. So I worked, and I worked hard, but I also went to clubs and got high and often found myself under the influence of various substances, which is to say, spiraling out of control, inside.

"Lord, I do not attempt to understand Your sublimity, because my intellect is not at all equal to such a task. But I yearn to understand some measure of Your truth, which my heart believes and loves. For I do not seek to understand in order to believe but I believe in order to understand. For I believe even this: that I shall not understand unless I believe."

Anselm of Canterbury
Benedictine Monk, Philosopher

So it was my time to believe, because I came to understand that the weapons of our warfare are not carnal. How does one find this out without reading the Word, and even after reading it, how does one come to understand fully?

> **"For the weapons of our warfare are not physical [weapons of flesh and blood], but they are mighty before God for the overthrow *and* destruction of strongholds, [Inasmuch as we] refute arguments *and* theories *and* reasonings and every proud *and* lofty thing that sets itself up against the [true] knowledge of God; and we lead every thought *and* purpose away captive into the obedience of Christ (the Messiah, the Anointed One)."**
>
> **2 Corinthians 10:4-5**

I would come to understand this very deeply. As quiet as it's kept, I am still learning. I'm sure that some probably only grasp a part of the meaning of this, "weapons of our warfare are not carnal," and how to activate it in the soul, in the heart, mind, thoughts, and mouth. I imagine that the worship leaders and intercessors I admire understand this—souls like T.D. Jakes, Martin Luther, Marvin Winans, Dr. Caroline Leaf, Billy Graham, Bam Crawford, Joyce Meyer, Beth Moore, Carroll A. Baltimore, Barbara William-Skinner, Robert Morris, Dr. Leonard N. Smith, Marcus Lamb, Matt Crouch, and many others. And I suspect that they, like myself, have had to overcome doubts, torments and anguish in order to understand it all more deeply.

7

DISCOVERING SEXUALITY AND GOALS AFTER TRAUMA

"Let fall in showers, you heavens, from above, and let the skies rain down righteousness [the pure, spiritual, heaven-born possibilities that have their foundation in the holy being of God]; let the earth open, and let them [skies and earth] sprout forth salvation, and let righteousness germinate *and* spring up [as plants do] together; I the Lord have created it."

Isaiah 45:8

I left Las Vegas, where I had endured yet been trafficked and seasoned and turned out for the first time, and went back to Los Angeles, where I had been trafficked the second time. I took a job at a restaurant in Los Angeles, where I longed in my heart to be, where I had lived since I was four years old. Of course, it would take time to understand the damage that had been done to my soul, but I would eventually have to face it, whether I understood it fully or not.

I knew something was wrong with me, and I knew my own efforts to bury it weren't working. I had been in L.A. for a bit after getting my license to do hair. I eventually took a job as an assistant at a hair salon and began working out at the gym to try and get a healthier life on track.

I was very involved in sports before and just after the first, early rape, and had always loved athletics. I was actually the first girl in an all-boys Little League in California. I was the pitcher, and I also played shortstop.

There were reporters and cool stuff like that when I pitched my first game, and I was on the cover of a Lake Elsinore newspaper. Our team came in first place, but I was not allowed to go to the state all-stars because girls were not allowed. This was heartbreaking at the time. I was also a straight "A" student before the rape, but as you already know, much changed after that.

When I escaped the life of child sex slavery, I made a life in L.A. I eventually went to acting school and did hair on the side. My relationship with my mother was not good at all, as too much had happened between us.

I was angry with her and my father, and I am sure they were angry with me. I was also very angry with the two stepfathers I had who had left and who were very violent to my mother. Was there a male figure in the world that stayed—actually cared, had courage, and loved in the way I had imagined it as a little child?

I had a vivacious character, and I was speaking at eight months old, before I could walk. This is why I am so very passionate about children and teens and others who are perhaps chronologically older but slipped through the cracks in the save-the-children process and, tragically, never got the critical help they needed to survive, psychically, or heal and thrive.

I believe that children have a certain innate ability to sense and hear God. They are closer to the womb and thus the supernatural, after all. But when that is robbed, when we hurt them, and harm one another, life is stifled. Emotional growth is stunted, and the boys who become men and girls who become women wake up not knowing who or what they are.

"If we lose love and self-respect for each other,
this is how we finally die."

Maya Angelou
Author, Poet

The following Scriptures state,

"Then little children were brought to Jesus, that He might put His hands on them and pray; but the disciples rebuked those who brought them. But He said, 'Leave the children alone! Allow the little ones to come to Me, and do not forbid *or restrain or* hinder them, for of such [as these] is the kingdom of heaven *composed*.'"

Matthew 19:13-14

At that time the disciples came to Jesus and asked, "Who, then, is the greatest in the kingdom of heaven?" He went on to say:

"And He called a little child to Himself and put him in the midst of them, And said, Truly I say to you, unless you repent (change, turn about) and become like little children [trusting, lowly, loving, forgiving], you can never enter the kingdom of heaven [at all]. Whoever will humble himself therefore and become like this little child [trusting, lowly, loving, forgiving] is greatest in the kingdom of heaven. And whoever receives *and* accepts *and* welcomes one little child like this for My sake and

in My name receives *and* accepts *and* welcomes Me."

Matthew 18: 2-5

Jesus is saying that unless we become as a child and unless we person receive "one such child," they do not welcome Him. He is no longer speaking of a physical child only but also an adult who has surrendered to Him and is *His* child. Wow! I get to be His baby girl, and it's like starting over, like starting life for the first time!

THAT IS ALL I EVER WANTED

I think it's wonderful for you to journey with me and experience with me realizations that changed my whole life. These profound openings and turning points allowed me to see that we are all leveled in God's eyes; we are all special in our own unique way.

Get this: There is no one on the planet now, or will ever be, that is better than you! This, of course, also means that you are neither greater than another as well. But the point remains: you are all you need to be right now.

*

Actor Jon Voight, who is still my friend today, would assist me in honing in on goals I once dreamed as a small child. He regularly came to the restaurant where I worked.

As a matter of fact, I was in awe, seeing so many amazing performers there. I thought that was everyone's experience. Anyway, he ordered pancakes.

Jon is an incredible Academy Award-winning actor, filmmaker, and father of two very special children, Jamie and Angelina. Jamie is also an actor, and as you well know, Angelina Jolie is also an actress, film-writer, director, producer, and international humanitarian, as well as wife and mother of six children.

All I remember, when I eventually visited Jon, were his son's and daughter's photos over the fireplace and elsewhere in his home. I could tell that he loved his children very much. That was very special to me because I had not grown up with my dad and had always loved (as most kids and even adults do) to see a father's love expressed. Even if expressed in small ways, it bears an awesome power. When we do see fathers with their children, we, on the outside, often see the love more than their children do at times; so, often, there are complex family issues that block so much from being experienced.

Jon came in the restaurant often, and he asked me questions about where I was from. He said there was something different about me, and I remember thinking, “Really?” I was so messed up at the time, but he was serious, and he would become my first mentor, which I must say is very important on life's journey. He was so pure in his approach, and he was very kind and sincere. He invited me to another gathering at his house, which was surreal, and I sang and ate very good food. I was scared, though, and had a difficult time; but they were patient. I told him that besides being a scientist, I longed to be an actor, that as a small child I did it all of the time and was even in a play at school. I had no idea that his friendship would encourage me to dream bigger than I had, and past all that I had been through.

Sometime after that, he took me to Whoopie Goldberg's house. It was Whoopie's birthday, and I thought, “NO WAY! Me? I'm going to meet this amazing, delightful person?” When I entered the house, which was on the ocean, I was shaking. I stood in front of her familiar, loving, kind face, and I was in such a state! It was dreamy, as if it were not real. There were other people there, and I am sure they were important in their own right, but this beautiful Black lady named Whoopie Goldberg was standing in front of me.

For a moment even Jon disappeared, but only for a

moment. I went to the bathroom to breathe. I looked at myself in the mirror to see if I was real and if my face was still there. When I came out they were about to watch a DVD and Whoopie said, "Sit down, Brook." Many people were sitting around on chairs and big fluffy sofas, so I sat right down in front of them all, right in the middle of the floor. I had no idea that it might have been weird at the time, but looking back is another story entirely. Whoopie said, "Not there, Brook." I felt embarrassed, but at the same time I thought it as comfortable a place as any.

She could tell I was nervous, and when I stood up, she asked me if I wanted to see the house and showed me around. It was beautiful, like a palace, one of those homes I had only seen in magazines. The beach was below, over a small cliff. She showed me a couple of family photos and simply extended a true kindness that I have never forgotten. Whoopie is one of the persons on my journey who did not treat me badly, even though I am certain I was an oddball. She was very gracious.

As a matter of fact, when Dr. Beverly Bam Crawford ordained me, she said that many had probably written me off. But with God, all things are possible and, of course, no matter who... Writes You Off... it is God who never does! Our Lord simply says,

> **"I will never leave you nor forsake you."**
>
> **Hebrews 13:5 (KJV)**

It is incredible how God passionately reached out to the children of Israel in the Book of Isaiah simply to tell them in no uncertain terms to believe and trust Him and that there is no God but Him.

> **"For the sake of Jacob My servant, and of Israel My chosen, I have called you by your name. I have surnamed you, though you have not known Me. I**

am the Lord, and there is no one else; there is no God besides Me. I will gird *and* arm you, though you have not known Me."

Isaiah 45:4-5

I would have to get to a place where I would eventually not care what others thought, at least in an unhealthy way.

I would have to get to the place where I would believe in God not only for my initial salvation but for everything.

If my heart and brain were going to be rewired and my life restored as though no time had been lost (as I spoke of in the story of the landowner), then the Lord my God would have to be my source, and I would have to believe the impossible could happen.

I would have to lean in and confidently trust in Him, so much so that I could discover that my strength comes from Him, not from the broken soul that could only "*fake it to make it.*"

Our strength comes from the giver of life, not things or people or jobs, only Him. It was and is important for me to love and to receive love from others, but when we know that He is our very source and provider, we are truly worshiping Him in every way. Thus, our relationships with others can now be what they should be: reliant on His guidance.

Coming from what I dealt with, it was easy for me to see this in the process of Jesus' leading me to wholeness. But what about when we don't know or haven't discovered that we may have areas in our own hearts which need to be searched out?

What if we have unresolved pain and unforgivingness? Perhaps we feel unsatisfied with where we are and have a sense that there is more to life.

Maybe we have thought of doing a mission's trip to other countries but are still waiting and waiting.

Maybe we are pressed to pray for others or reach out and walk up to a stranger but often ask for others to do it because we are too close to the situation.

Maybe we have thought of starting our own business or doing things through the work that we do which have kingdom-building at the center. Perhaps we have knowledge that life is greater when we give and when our work somehow assists God with His, even if the way that we think seems small to us. Honestly, if it has come up in our hearts more than once or twice, it is more than likely the Holy Spirit.

GOD IS NO RESPECTER OF PERSONS

What a passionate and faithful God we serve! Yet I hadn't known Him, and because of the pain I was in, and in the severe brokenness of my heart and mind, I had not wanted to know Him. I had not wanted to trust Him, or anyone for that matter. I used to say, "If I ain't doing it, it ain't getting done." But that's not true at all, even though so many others agreed with me.

I walked into a church after being a victim of child sex slavery and because of the sin that was done to me, I felt out of place there. I was addicted to drugs and looking at the floor all of the time, because it was hard to stare into the faces of others. Some church-goers often saw this odd, confused, gay, lesbian, bisexual, self-realization-attending meditator trying to talk to God individually, and I'm sure many judged me. I'm sure they had no idea how serious I was, as are those of us who have been emptied, wanting to know and be filled with His love.

There is so much more to His love than I could have imagined. So, I stayed away from church in that season. It was difficult to take the stares without the smiles and friendly hellos. Nowadays, I look for those who I see really need to be encouraged, respected, and loved for who they are, and I let them know about God's amazing Grace! But what did the Lord think and say as He spoke in the following Scriptures?

"And the scribes [belonging to the party] of the Pharisees, when they saw that He was eating with [those definitely known to be especially wicked] sinners and tax collectors, said to His disciples, 'Why does He eat *and drink* with tax collectors and [notorious] sinners?' And when Jesus heard it, He said to them, 'Those who are strong *and* well have no need of a physician, but those who are weak *and* sick; I came not to call the righteous ones *to repentance*, but sinners (the erring ones and all those not free from sin).'"

Mark 2:16-17

I surmise here that the battlefield of the mind, my mind, has been a life's journey and didn't even begin until I exposed my mind, my heart, to the Master and Creator of it. Eventually, I had to learn to keep my eyes on my prize, my miracle, which was and is the Lord Himself, and not to look at their faces nor to the left or to the right in comparison.

I had no idea that after what I went through, I could have a relationship with a real God, a true God, and I want for others to know how real it is. But that is just what God desired for you before the foundations of the world (Romans 8).

It was a sunny and easy day in Los Angeles, California, and I had been struggling with so many addictions. I was also struggling with my sexuality, because I knew I wasn't born that way and that it was not an issue until after the abuse. So, for those who feel they were born that way, I am not speaking about you. I can only speak for myself, and I was slowly different because some traumatic things happened.

Even though I did not know the Lord as I do now, nor was I born anew, I was seeking. In the process of seeking, God spoke to me and visited me in dreams, and I knew that I did not want to involve myself with anyone physically anymore, male or female, to be honest. I just needed to STOP and focus my heart on God and healing, because physical relations often confuse reality.

I did not understand fornication, nor did I understand that I had a choice in stopping without thinking something was wrong with me. When you have only lived by the standards and dictates of twisted and perverted norms, you don't always understand that God has laid out amazing choices for us, and through them we can become new!

It is through these choices, which are a part of the "narrow road" of which Scriptures speak, that we are healed. Scripture says that it would be easier for a camel to enter the eye of a needle than for the rich to enter the kingdom of God. "The rich" implies those who have the world as their god and have their faith in the dictates of the flesh and mere worldly desires. This means not taking this amazing, courageous journey along the road of the narrow path.

I knew that I had to stop having sex once I was out of the brothel experience and just try to live life, stop going out, stop everything to be able to discover something new. I felt horrible during and after the acts, acts that were part of my subconscious heart and mind but not part of my hopes or my dreams.

How could I overcome and get through something that was such a part of my being, so interwoven in the fabric of who I had become?

There was obviously no love in any of it, as it had a type of brokenness to it.

I am not saying that homosexual couples don't love one another in the way that they do, but I also know it [the attraction] can be rooted in self-image because it is the same sex, after all.

I also know that God is love, and unless we love as He has, various stages in our lives can be hard to understand; so we must care for others regardless of where they are or who they are, for that matter.

There were simply lines, avenues, and bridges, so to speak, which were not God's best for me to cross over anymore. I knew I wanted to marry a man one day, and that personally, for me, my homosexuality was based on fear and familiarity.

It was *fabulous* and *fierce* as they say, or was it? I eventually would leave all of that "fabulousness" behind, all of that vainglory of sex and the confusion that I felt, to pursue the Glorious One!

I just knew it was not for me, and I never had an opportunity to choose for myself due to the violent abuse I had received. We have to be very patient and loving with kids who are uncertain about their sexuality.

In addition to all this, there was a constant hunger to be loved through the physical act of lust. I am not saying that sex in or out of marriage does not satisfy the flesh, but without the love of God, what is it really? In marriage it takes on a supernatural form of wonder, which can only be found in knowing the Lord and trusting Him and Him alone.

I also began to understand that the word *sex* at its root means *intimacy.* According to Greek Roots, found on Wikipedia, the Greek word for intimacy is *koinonia.* "The share, which one has in anything, participation, a gift jointly contributed, a collection, a contribution, etc. It identifies the idealized state of fellowship and unity that should exist within the Church, the Body of Christ. The essential meaning of the *koinonia* embraces concepts conveyed in the English terms community, communion, joint participation, sharing and intimacy."[1]

It is innately our desire to know and be known, and ultimately to be known by God! That is a POWERFUL statement because it shines the light on our deep need to be loved.

Sex was never meant to be for sport, to pass the time, or to be casual. I believe it was created for the exciting aspects of life in action and moving forward in family, creating with God as we meet and spend our lives with that special someone.

The enemy places in our midst constant distractions from the true road to love's discovery, which is found in healthy relationships.

Our culture pushes taking care of oneself to the point of dysfunction, and this makes it difficult for some survivors to know who they were born to be. Especially, when our overly sexualized society grooms youth to exploit or be exploited. Oftentimes, we deal with the symptoms of sexual orientation, for instance, by trying to evaluate them based on a cultural worldly outlook about what is okay, what is healthy, and what is acceptable, as opposed to what is Godly and what is earnestly sustainable and rooted in love and truth.

Is who you are okay, and what, exactly, means you are not? Sometimes this is why many victims are not soaring beyond, because it can be difficult to find the answers; it was for me.

Worldly clinicians, without standard or gauge except for current cultural acceptance, sometimes lead us astray with various theories of sexuality and choice. But what does God say? Because most victims have been near death or truly died and are trying to discover life, we know that there is more; we've seen so much already, including the dark side of a lot of it!

We realize that some of the cultural trails and roads the world has taken have structural damage because we were in the heart of its ills and the depths of its ugliness. We've seen way down the rabbit hole, and we've lived there.

We've seen some stuff that, regardless of what we come to believe, lets us know there is a place called hell.

Because we are on the other side of it, we also know that there is something more. Andrew Comiskey, a former homosexual who also discovered he was not born homosexual nor desired to be that way, says this in an interview: "That cannot happen via a 50-minute session once a week. We need BOTH—the incisive nature of the therapeutic relationship, combined with a community of shared, counter-cultural values. I think both are non-negotiable. We must work hard to try and ensure both for those who are gradually walking out of their same-sex attraction."[2]

This is exactly the powerful thing the Lord had given me: a counter-cultural point of view, right from the creator of heaven and earth, of who I needed to be and who I desired and longed to be, regardless of what my broken emotions exuded at that time. For those of you who feel you were born that way and that is and was your life's choice, this passage is not for you, nor am I judging you. But I knew I wanted something different; I knew that my sexuality did not include lesbianism. But how could I shake off the childhood rape and fear experiences and trauma which had occurred by no choice of mine?

What I would feel in mere emotions would not come to matter when the burning desire of the love of God was within me. It was time to lay down my weapons and trust Him..

"In war, when a commander becomes so bereft of reason and perspective that he fails to understand the dependence of arms on Divine guidance, he no longer deserves victory."

Lucius Annaeus Seneca
Roman Stoic Philosopher, Statesman

With God, the mysteries of life and creation are revealed to us. Scriptures say they are only revealed to those who are His.

Of course, that includes ANYBODY who desires a relationship with God, but for those who do not, the Word is clear that those mysteries are hidden from them.

"And He replied to them, 'To you it has been given to know the secrets *and* mysteries of the kingdom of heaven, but to them it has not been given."

Matthew 13:11

Having been trafficked by heterosexual pimps as well as by "normal" married men, the way former victims view things is different. Unfortunately, this also gives us a first-hand opportunity to understand much more than those who've not been trafficked about the twisted nature of our society today. Homosexual or not, many of us survivors have extreme and distorted views about what is sexually okay and what is not. We are evidently in a dark age, where recent statistics conclude that over 60 percent of adult men look at pornography[3]—albeit, in the order of things, women sometimes follow.

Nonetheless, I knew I wanted more than that. I wanted what I read about at creation, and I desired the pure virtuousness of God in my life. I had not known it would be as a Christian, as most Christians I had met at that time did not seem to possess the illumination of love and the light of the glory of God that Jesus Himself preached. I also thought at one point that I would go to Hebrew school but realized that I can have both as a Judeo-Christian.

I eventually understood that just because some didn't have that truly loving light, that didn't mean it wasn't there. I've always thought that the Mystical Movement had distorted Biblical things; thus, when we as believers see some of it, we cling to that partial truth and close our eyes to the rest.

The rainbow, which some use to declare their freedom; the stones in the "breast plate of righteousness"; meditation on the Word in a quiet place and words like *energy*, which only means *electricity* or *power*—all partake of the supernatural and the scientific nature of God.

So, I thought I'd find a different faith, perhaps some form that seemed easy or friendlier. And, to be frank, not a form of religion created by White men, where Black slaves, of which I am a descendant, were brainwashed!

I was glad to know man did not create Chistianty at all, nor can it be his design. I'm sharing this because I speak to many about this and for the record, Jesus wasn't White or Black either. He didn't have blonde hair and blue eyes or long, straight hair. I doubt if anyone did in that part of the world at that time. And all of these incomprehensible arguments between Christians were troublesome to me because, at the heart, it really doesn't matter. I imagine He was somehow everything and everyone. Of course, it does get complicated with man! But truth is never complicated in God and His awesome love for us!

Many of the believers I had met came with rigid judgments and sermons which were not filled with the compassion that Jesus had when He sat before those who the religious folks said were hypocrites (I'm not speaking of fake friendliness or empty smiles, anyone can do that). You see, when you've been in the thick of it, you learn some things about people. You learn about darkness and when it's present; you can sense it. I do realize that is slowly changing in the Church, and I am so glad about it because unity is what God is all about. It's time we end the separateness in the Church and try to come together. But that's me, the ultimate optimist.

I was already a unique child. I had dreams and visions which I did not understand and ideas to do things differently, but much of my life had been spent in brokenness. That is why I desire freedom for others. Darkness came in and robbed me for a time, as with many children and adults, but even in that I know that God is getting His best out of me now.

If I had it to do over again, I do not know what I would change, if anything, because I celebrate His creation and creative power in me today. This is the irony within pain and tragedy.

That is what I long for, for so many people—young, mature, and elder. My hope is that we simply do not look back as I used to do, but look ever forward and reach back only to grab from the arsenal of all we have learned. This is just as King David did when he fought Goliath. Look at this with me, Beloved:

> **"Now Eliab his eldest brother heard what he said to the men; and Eliab's anger was kindled against David and he said, 'Why did you come here? With whom have you left those few sheep in the wilderness? I know your presumption and evilness of heart; for you came down that you might see the battle.' And David said, 'What have I done now? Was it not a harmless question?'"**
>
> **1 Samuel 17:28-29**

Look at that! Now, we have heard the sermons, but there is always the need to ponder and reflect on the Word of God no matter how many times we read it. The Holy Spirit, at different times and seasons in our lives, will give us revelations we have not heard or will refresh like a beautiful spring morning the things and lessons we have. How did I apply this experience of David to my own life and in my struggle?

There is too much to write, but read the entire Book of 1 Samuel. I can clearly see here "that we wrestle not against flesh and blood," and, with all that David accomplished later in life, that this day was a divine appointment!

One of his elder brothers was trying to stop the victory, not only for David but also for Israel. It is often people we love and who should love us that hurt us the most. His brother was even going against God's plans and purpose.

We see the promise of David's life was of God. What that means is when you keep your eyes on the unique journey that God has brought and is bringing you through, and when you remember how He has kept you, whether you are just discovering it now or not, you can rest assured that He has the wherewithal to bring you all the way to glory!

I have often had to get to a quiet place, even in tears, to fight the thoughts of failure and the anguish of self-loathing. There have even been the fleshly desires which I had to cast down until eventually they stayed away. Be encouraged!

After all, I felt like my feminine parts were trash, that they had been used for trash such as foreign sperm, urine, and objects. The womb is the center of a woman's body, a sacred place. But with rape and sexual violence being so common, there are many women who find it normal to have an *angry vagina.* This broken woman and womb that Adam in scripture once called "life spring." (Genesis 3:20) But if now man trashes and rapes what he once called, Eve; which means "the mother of all living," what does that speak to society and creation? It says, destruction and self has become more important than building and unity. Because I am, as is everyone, attached to every part of my body, yet and still, my flesh cannot rule and reign, and so my soul had to die to self. That means that each day I have to remind myself that God is in control.

I was in a car accident many years ago, in which we hit a car head-on, and my teeth were already cracked, unfortunately when I was beat up it was much easier with the hard blow for my teeth to be knocked out.

The person driving the car I was in was a radical, blonde-haired party girl, and we were out of it (luckily no one was hurt but us). That was how life was and somewhere inside I knew I had to find a way out. When I stared in the mirror at my bloody drunk face with no teeth I had no idea that I could come back to life - back to whatever destiny God had always had for me, even before I was born.

I loved science as a young girl, as I said, and to take apart things and put them together. You see, I had a desire to uncover, to understand the mysteries of life at a young age.

When I was in first grade, a friend of my mother's came to the house. She told me all about cancer and that she had breast cancer. She shared how painful the experience was for her. I was six and a half years old and listened closely to this beautiful woman, understood somehow, and felt her pain. I walked her to her car and I believed somehow that she could be healed, but I didn't understand what that meant. I am sure you also can look back at times when God was sharing with you at a very young age some of these very same impressions in your spirit.

Darkness knew that one day I would no longer be locked in that prison. He could tell by the questions I was asking, and I am sure by the statistics he uses.

It would take me years with God to heal, and I would eventually find myself walking along the path, led by the Lord and not by everything else.

The realm of the demonic may not know the future, but they know the past from creation. They use statistics and mathematics, as well as experience from all that we say and do. They can see heaven's entire host, who have always surrounded us, and who they are; and by that, they can calculate our divine calling, along with our God-given gifts and our abilities, which they have studied. But thank you, Lord, for your keeping Grace through it all!

Prayer Corner

The Prayers of the righteous avail much...
Oh, Father, we thank you for your mercy, your tender and long-suffering ways. For every reader, dear God, I pray for salvation. I pray for your marvelous hands to cover them gently and with divine strength, pull them ever closer to you—hidden beneath your wings, your mighty pinions, my God! Let God be true and every man in error all for your Glory and the benefits of salvation in their lives, God. I thank you for the deliverance from sexual sin done to them, from the ills of being victims, witnesses, or perpetrators of these horrific crimes. Father, I know and realize that you and you alone are the ultimate answer, and have all of the answers, and I pray

that your supernatural voice and presence will visit each one as they read this prayer right now so they will be led to the right help in every area of their lives, even the right therapist and church, temple, or synagogue, Lord God, if they need it! That even as they go through their day and night, in and out of sleep, that you will make your omniscient presence known unto them like never before and even for the first time!

Father, I ask that you will rewire minds and hearts in perfect healing, for your Glory needs to be revealed in such a way. Lord, every girl, woman, child or man that has been trafficked, raped, and pillaged be released, healed, and set free on every level! I thank you for transformed minds and lives! Father, whatever time was spent in the fire of abuse, according to your Word in the story of the landowner, I ask and thank you that nothing is missed in their destiny! You are the true and only Restorer, oh heavenly Abba Father, shine your light of Glory on them in a powerful and majestic way today, God! Let their lives never, ever, be the same again. I thank you for supernatural favor, grace, and mental soundness now, in Your unmatchable name. Amen!

Part 3

Salvation Is Freedom Often Experienced in the Presence of Unrest

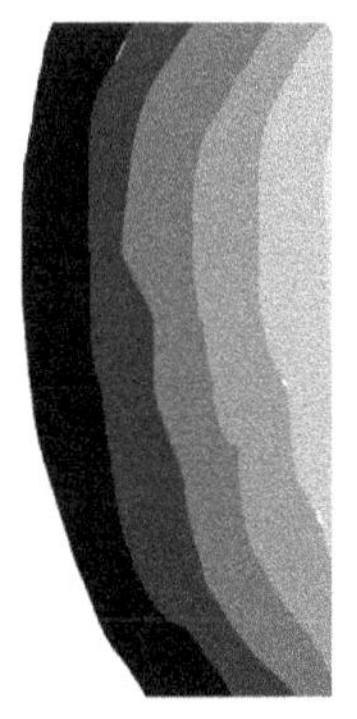

8

THE GREATEST GIFTS COME AFTER DEFEAT

Salvation is not the gift from a God who does not care about our well-being nor for the poor in the earth who have nothing better, as some writers and speakers have said. It is the reason for life's existence. It is the challenge already won by the Savior of which only true warriors and people of courageous trust can enter into. It is true enlightenment, it is before all ever was, before there was ever an earth.

Christianity is not new; it was at creation with God the Creator, the great I Am who sent His Son, in the flesh, who was already in existence with Him at creation. It has been called many things and exploited by those who came in its name with falsehood. Nevertheless, it is real, it is powerful, and it saved my life and keeps on saving it. Moreover, the supernatural appointments in a so-called chance meeting and in extraordinary moments can lead to the fulfillment of destiny, if only we are mature enough in heart to listen, hear, and understand.

I had lunch with actor Jon Voight, which was another learning experience. These times began to lead me on an amazing path. We met at a favorite restaurant of his in Studio City, and I mentioned to him that I was searching for God, that I needed to know who God was because I felt so much missing in my life.

I had been dating, if you will, this well-known singer of a band (which I will not name), and I told her that I had a dream that shook me in a good way. It was more like a vision or visitation, but I could not explain it. She told me it sounded like I was on LSD and laughed. Isn't it funny how we, when broken, cling to others who we know in our heart of hearts do not love us nor truly care about our well-being?

We can see that they are moved by what we can do for them, and not much else. Even then, I got so tired of hearing curse words and being in places where dark spirits lived and got fat. I was conditioned to ignore the obvious, and that is what many young people go through today. In the vision, and I think, heavenly encounter, I was in another place, heaven, I think.

The air was clean; the sun had a type of brightness that I had not experienced. I had flown overseas and touched the water and soared. In this place, I walked along a surreal green meadow. It was filled with beauty.

There were beautiful trees and flowers as far as the eye could see. Suddenly, a huge lion was walking beside me. He was so big that we were almost the same height, even though He walked on four legs as lions do. But this lion was warm, and the love that exuded from him was indescribable.

We were talking to each other, yet our mouths never moved; it was incredible. I began to feel thirsty and suddenly the lion asked me to wait.

I stopped and he walked into a forest nearby, coming back with a cup in his mouth filled with water. It was a cup that he could hang from his teeth. In the vision, I held my head back, and the lion poured water into my mouth. I was no longer thirsty, and I was filled with joy! In another dream, I was in a similar meadow, and I was dancing in it alongside fruit trees of various kinds.

As I danced on this bright and sunny day, the sun way up in the sky began to move to the same beat as me, as though we were dancing together! I was shocked and started to become silly and overjoyed. All of a sudden, the sun flew from the sky and lay on its back right in front me. It started to play as though it was an innocent puppy or child laughing! It was crazy!

I took citrus fruits from the nearby trees, broke them open, and squeezed the juice of the fruit into the sun. He laughed and laughed with such a big loud sound that when I woke up from this vision, my jaws hurt.

After we played and laughed for a while (without speaking out loud), he told me he had to go back up in the sky; it was like he was saying not to worry. This is what I dreamed before I came to Christ.

It was not long after, that I left the singer and began to discover how to be what I call a "late-blooming virgin," a new virgin. This was right before my chat with Jon and about seven months before I would become a Christian.

My journey to becoming a Christian started with several months at the Self-Realization Fellowship.

Jon didn't know what I needed then, but he knew I needed something bigger than myself.

Before I'd had therapy or anything like that, Jon mentioned this amazing place in Pacific Palisades called the Self-Realization Fellowship, a worldwide spiritual organization founded by Paramahansa Yogananda in 1920 and based in Mount Washington in Los Angeles, California. It is registered in California as a religious organization. He mentioned it because it was interdenominational and they invite you no matter what you believe, even if it was nothing, and that sounded like me.

So I went. It is a stunning location a few blocks from Malibu Beach and nestled in a crest of beautiful gardens off the long winding road of Sunset Boulevard, which ends at Pacific Coast Highway, one of my favorite places on the planet.

They have more than one location, and I would find out later that there was a photo at one of the locations in which Paramahansa Yogananda was giving my great-great-uncle, John Somerville, a special award in Los Angeles, in the mid- to late-1930s. John was also a dentist who was married to my grandfather's aunt, Vada Watson-Somerville, who was the first African American woman to graduate from U.S.C. Dental School and be licensed in California. John was the second.

Nonetheless, I went on a Sunday to one of the services. The seating was both inside and outside, and I chose to sit outside in the open air and sunshine.

I honestly was so happy to be there, I really wanted so much to be with God. On the altar inside, there are several photos, including ones of Kryshna, Paramahansa Yogananda, and Jesus Christ, with their names written below.

Now, I knew both then and now that all of the photos of Jesus are not accurate, and we really don't know much except He had hair of wool and that we, according to Scripture, do not know Him "after the flesh" (2 Corinthians 5:16, KJV). But, excitingly, the photo of Him stood out. Back when I was nine years old or so, I went to a Roman Catholic Church with my then stepfather and asked to be baptized. I also did my first communion and knew then that God was real. But life happened, and I had not gotten to know God after everything I experienced. So I was glad to see the photo at this center.

I looked around at the multicultural crowd. I felt safe, which was a big thing for me because I was uncomfortable in most places, and they seemed nice enough.

The speaker, who was wearing a long robe, was a steely White man with a soft face and buzzed and balding hair; he used some Scripture from the Bible in the sermon. I was very drawn to these because he spoke about love and acceptance. Afterward, I took a stroll in the garden, as many did, and studied the Scriptures as I read about meditation in the Word.

It was a great day and the first time I heard the Scripture "Be still and know that I Am God" (Psalm 46:10, KJV). I think I kind of knew that stillness was not just in prayer and would be something I would learn to capture no matter where I was. It would also become part of my meditation time with God. It stood out to me that day but also in all that I would do.

I went to the bookstore and bought the book *The Autobiography of a Yogi*, by Paramahansa Yogananda, and I loved it. It stood out in their bookstore, which also sold Bibles.

It explained to me for the first time that God was real and that He loved me and wanted to know me or, rather, for me to know Him. It was filled with tons of Bible Scriptures as well. It also let me know that the "impossible is possible" with the Lord. He used the name of Jesus in the book, and I was very moved by that.

In the life of this man, you might have thought he was a Christian, with all of that, as his journey was his coming-of-age story. That was the interesting part, in a way, because I couldn't tell. I certainly did not know whether he was or he wasn't; but what I did know was that, even though I loved the book, as I love to read, I knew that Jesus was more than a prophet. I knew He was the beloved Son of God, but I didn't understand it all yet and began to ask God what it all meant.

I would come to the Fellowship often and even bring a new friend whom I had met at a local club, because she seemed to be searching too. It was nice because she didn't judge me nor I, her. She fell in love with the place as I did.

After one of the services, I asked the speaker if being homosexual was okay. I didn't want to hurt all the model/actress girlfriends I knew. I didn't want to hurt anyone; I just needed to know because they continued to call and call, even though I was running in the other direction. His answer was that "this was an unusual and difficult vibration, and there are easier roads to travel." I really didn't understand at the time, but I think it was a good answer for me because I did know that my life had to change.

I was dating Guy Laliberté, the president and founder of *Cirque Du Soleil,* and I was certainly deeply in love with him. I know he cared for me deeply as well, but I was so afraid that I did not know how to handle real love. Isn't that a peculiar phrasing, "real love"? As if there is one that is false.

"How else but through a broken heart may Christ enter in?"

Oscar Wilde
Writer, Poet

I realize now, after perceiving on some level how amazing the Father's love is for the Son, how amazing their love is for us. Even the Holy Spirit—how His presence is always with us and strong when we yield and take heed to seek, and spend time, and listen…how beautiful it really is. Knowing Jesus like I do, I understand the love that He has for the Father and us in order for Him to bear our burdens. To be spit on by a huge garrison of big, mean, cruel men and to be cut, bruised beyond recognition, buffeted by evil over and over again, and still love them, and us?

There is nothing else but this kind of love, because God is the creator of it and anything else is a poor, malfunctioning, imaginary, bad counterfeit. I think what is so powerful is that we don't have to try and love like Jesus; all we have to do is love Him because the rest has already been taken care of through Him. In the next passage the writer refers to "survivors," and it really moved me:

> **"Assemble yourselves and come; draw near together, you survivors of the nations! They have no knowledge who carry about [in religious processions or into battle] their wooden idols and keep on praying to a god that cannot save."**
>
> **Isaiah 45:20**

When I think of this gift now, I see why darkness pursues, keeping us from it and its ill repute.

I know I am sidetracking here, because to me, we are having a conversation, even though you are reading or listening. But I have written this testimony for Jesus and you.

In this conversation, as in most, I am prompted to have these memories and revelations surface from the center of my heart while I am in the middle of sharing something else. I hope you don't mind, Beloved, because I desire for us to take the rest of this journey together. As I write, I am thinking of you with God's love!

I long for you to know how special and gifted you are. I long for you to be enlightened and illuminated by the Glory of God—the very same Glory that raised up Jesus the Christ from the dead. I long for you to be a free-thinker and to live the life of freedom that He came, died, and rose for you to have, regardless of your past.

Your times are now or can be in the Master's loving hands and tended to by His grace. Halleljah! Thank you, God! I'm laughing and smiling now with joy from the healing miracles that are taking place as you read this.

Faith does come by hearing (even if reading and hearing in your heart or reading out loud like I do sometimes, especially Scriptures), the Word of God.

After all I had been through, however, I began to believe just a little that one day, I could really discover who I was born to be. I got to a place where I enjoyed learning about others. It was as if I would look *through* others, trying to find truth and authenticity. That's what's so interesting about the time I was homeless. It seems as though there are so many homeless people who have lost so much for so many reasons that you find folks who resonate passion, even if just for moments at a time. It is incredible that most of them just wanted to be loved, and most were broken from different forms of abuse. I was, as are many survivors of all kinds whom I've met, in houses of bondage emotionally after the physical ones. We escaped, major trauma, yet it remained so deeply rooted in many of our actions.

People said I seemed aloof and distant. I felt like a little girl in a grown-up world and a grown-up body. I was twenty-something, but honestly I felt like I was 12 on one end and 99 on the other. Part of my heart and mind stopped blossoming, and there was no individuality to my outlook about myself or others but I longed for more.

I did sometimes sense and know that there was more, and if I could sit still long enough, I would capture glimpses of what could be. But I realized that at the "point of impact," as I said earlier, I stopped healthy growth patterns in my heart connection in many aspects; and a part of me was already dying. But God says that I am raised up with Christ (Ephesians 2:6; Colossians 2:12). I knew that if I could just keep moving forward, something would happen. Then I could finally experience being raised up with Jesus. This would mean death to my past, death to all that ailed my soul. Because if He could leave the grave clothes in the tomb, and I was raised with Him to live this life, then I could, too—if I only knew how. I had already been giving up on the most important thing without ever knowing it, and that was who I was meant to be. Scripture says:

> **"Be strong and courageous. Do not fear or be in dread of them, for it is the LORD your God who goes with you. He will not leave you or forsake you."**
>
> **Deuteronomy 31:6**

I was trying to be strong, trying to push past the past, but I had never shared it with anyone in full. The Lord was saying the strength in me was only part of it. "It is nothing without wisdom and understanding," He said, "because when you go through life, you try so hard to be strong, daughter. It is futile because I have already done it for you, and now it's how you view it all." The Bible says:

> **"If the foundations be destroyed what will the righteous do?"**
>
> **Psalms 11:3 (KJV)**

Herein, I begin to lay out how God supernaturally has come in to pull up the old foundation, which creates a stony and broken heart, to lay a new one. Scripture states:

> **"Train up a child in the way he should go [and in keeping with his individual gift or bent], and when he is old he will not depart from it."**
>
> **Proverbs 22:6**

It is true that children have to be led according to the natural abilities that parents, if whole themselves, can notice with God's guidance. Unfortunately, that is often not the case. In addition, when you train up a child in a corrupt environment of abuse, what does this create in them? When I came to Jesus, He became my teacher, my trainer.

Through the Word of God, with the help of mentors along the way that hear from Him, He took me as His little child and began the work of this Scripture in my life on new levels. It does not matter what age you are; you are God's child, His precious angel, and He loves you like no other!

> **"The LORD is my strength and my shield; in him my heart trusts, and I am helped; my heart exults, and with my song I give thanks to him."**
>
> **Psalms 28:7**

When I think of the backbone of the power of how God has created the human heart and mind and its connection to the divine, I am awestruck on how loved we really are. And for my heart to exult Him as David has written, I would have to experience, for myself, the perpetual love of God that does transform!

Oftentimes, when I speak, I think of so many parallels in life and profound points in history such as slavery, or the civil rights movement; I wonder how we take all of this knowledge from these experiences in our history and really preach and teach or what I like to say, "treach" messages that really rally our youth and bridge build between cultures, just here in America for starters.

We often discriminate because we think we know who someone is, and often we're so wrong, and God is the only one who is right. So, I began a journey to try and understand others.

In the documentary film I shot in the Middle East to try and discover what some of the world thinks about freedom and human rights, which depicts some aspects of my journey and that of others, I was fortunate to hear the Holy Spirit specifically guide me to do something that I in no way thought I could do.

LESSONS IN UNLIKELY PLACES AT UNLIKELY TIMES

I traveled to Dubai and the Kingdom of Bahrain so that I could document so many cultures and people in a few places from all over the world and what they thought about rape, freedom, human rights and so on, I even was part of a baptism in the Persian Gulf in the middle of the night as it had to be done in secret. But I had the opportunity to go to Bahrain and the catch was that in order to film at a specific ceremony that I had never heard of I had to go undercover. One thing I had came to understand when going undercover in the Kingdom of Bahrain occurred during the *Arbaeen* ceremony. *Arba'een*, Arabic (الأربعين) for *forty* or *Chehelom*, Persian (چهلم) or Urdu (چہلم) for *the fortieth* [day], is a Shia Muslim religious observance which occurs 40 days after the Day of *Ashura.* It commemorates the martyrdom of Hussein bin Al.[1]

During this time, there were thousands of men and women present. The men in walkways, the streets, and pathways would chant, while women in black watched with babies in their arms. I hadn't understood until afterwards that going as an American undercover was extremely dangerous. A member of the Marines, a Colonel in fact, told me I could have never been heard from again. I knew, however, that the Lord had called me there, and as I depicted in my documentary film *Survivor,* blood splattered onto my face while I watched the brutal cuts and slashes the people inflicted on their backs and bodies.

As I saw a man who was bleeding to death and the shredded skin on others' backs, I thought of freedom. Given the right circumstances, we would do anything to find it. In that moment, standing there in the street in Bahrain, far from my American home and surrounded by Muslims, I felt compassion.

As part of my healing journey from abuse, the Lord showed me what I had done to myself. The psychological damage that I lived under was worse than I thought. I had slashed and harmed myself and tried to inflict more pain on my own life and soul, as they were doing by beating themselves until they were very marred.

That is what we do when we operate in fear and worry, we torture ourselves.

Many victims of abuse—even sometimes children who grow up in broken homes, men, boys who are raped, women who are raped, those who grow up with various kinds of emotional abuse—will often beat themselves up in other ways. Drug addiction was one way that I did. Another was self-loathing and the sabotaging of dreams, even and especially after I was born again. Some teens use cutting as a means to self-mutilate. I just didn't think I was worthy. I became very good, as many victims of abusive backgrounds do, at reading the gesticulations and body language of those around me. Because science has determined that 70 percent of communication is nonverbal,[2] which is how we learn, I could see and sense what others thought. When you don't know who you are in life, this can send you into an uneasy life every day of the week! We don't ever see our own faces but merely a reflection of them, and often that reflection is in the eyes of others. We are to look for and seek the face of Jesus and reach for Him because His eyes are always filled with love.

"It is not so true that 'prayer changes things' as that prayer changes me and I change things. God has so constituted things that prayer on the basis of Redemption alters the way in which a man looks at things. Prayer is not a question of altering things externally, but of working wonders in a man's disposition."

Oswald Chambers
Evangelist, Writer, Teacher

9

BEING TRANSFORMED: SPIRIT AND SCIENCE PLAY A PART

"The human heart feels things the eyes cannot see, and knows what the mind cannot understand."

Robert E. Valett
Author

Earlier in the book, I spoke a bit on the truth that we are a spirit. We live in a body and we have a soul, a soul that comprises our will, our mind, our emotions, and our ability to maneuver in and around who we are. When people hear the word *sex*, something happens in the brain-heart-body connection that can cause confusion for others and ourselves in the outcome.

For years, I was confused about my sexuality because someone had assassinated my soul. For years, I was confused by so many things such as boundaries, because in a trafficked situation they are not the same as in society. The way a child in slavery gets a picture of the world is from the viewpoint of the true side of evil, so that often, as we go through life afterward, we see it in others. We are able to spot things that others can't see. Communication is mostly nonverbal, and in a brothel, or in horrific circumstances in general, victims are not allowed to talk very much at all. As a result, we get very keen on discerning the soul and the spirit in operation, and most times we don't even realize how good we've become in doing this until much later.

So, we know very well when someone on *this* side of it, when we are in counseling and such, is assisting us *because they really care* or *because of other, less sincere reasons*. We can see it. We are also very good at reading gestures and all forms of body language, as I said.

This is good and bad. What it means is that when a police officer or other first responder has a lust issue and is trying to help us, we shut down, turn away, or just play him because we see the issue.

We also can read between the lines when people are overly religious and want to pray and lay hands on us quickly without really listening.

The Bible says:

"Lay hands on no man suddenly."

1 Timothy 5:22 (KJV)

We may deal with their actions because we have no place to go, but parts of our minds and hearts are not in it.

We also see when women who are well-meaning have many broken issues in their lives. They are in and out of the Church and trying to assist victims; we see that it lets them "have a life," so to speak, and that's okay, but often they work without having ever dealt with their own issues, which we can also sense.

Survivors like myself need to know that we are no longer orphans, and that we are accountable. If I say I'm going to be somewhere, then I am, especially when a victim or survivor is recently rescued. The root word for *orphan* in Greek also means *fatherless*, and I was one of these kids who did not have my father as I was growing up. Even with Mom there, a child can still be orphaned to this degree, as a father's presence is an extraordinary thing. Children are best and happy when raised and loved by their parents or by loving guardians. I'm going to speak in the next chapter on the importance of fathers and give some astounding statistics on what can happen when a father is absent.

You see, we don't always understand how much God the *Father* loves us because in most situations, receiving His love and trusting him is difficult for survivors.

Other times older survivors who are over 21 profess that God has been there all the while, but they are still searching to understand Him more, as I did, to receive all that life in Him offers. And what most believers desire from Him after all, is everything.

Survivors like myself do need to heal, but in the process of healing they also need food, love, shelter, and the knowledge that someone will be there and not give up on them.

I love the section in the Scriptures in which Jesus fed the multitudes before he gave the Word, so they could hear clearly all that He had to impart. He fed their spirits, souls, *and* their bodies.

The Scriptures speak about growing our faith, about imitating God and good (Ephesians 5), about being diligent, for whether bound or free, there is a reward for being diligent.

For victims to become survivors and survivors to become thrivers and thrivers to become champions we must grow our faith, whatever that means to us at the time, we must learn to be other centered which is imitating God and so much more and then we will begin to experience first hand our own transformation.

The muscles produced in the process of a developing life in this violent situation are, in fact, built awry. Thus, we wake up with the diligent habits related to thoughts such as "I don't need anybody," "I can do it on my own," "No one can be trusted," "All he wants is sex," and other questionable and damaging mindsets.

The other side of this is that the brothel experience is so

clearly dark that there is often a sweet naïveté to survivors later on.

Sometimes, people look at survivors as being savvy when it comes to the world, and that's true but not in all areas. When a survivor is *out* of the violent situation, we are sometimes *more* innocent and *more* naïve, because at first we assume that if *you* say you love us, it's true, even if we can see you have your own issues.

Just like an innocent child, we give you the benefit of the doubt because now we are in a world that we wanted to be a part of for so long, a world that we were outside of, looking in. This was for so long a world that we thought would be filled with love, truth, nice fluffy beds and cookies and families around the TV eating popcorn. We longed for that—for family.

In this book, we are having a conversation about a life born from ashes of despair becoming a dream come true and wondering how we take part in our own dreams. You see, I began to study the brain and heart a decade ago. But I am not a neurobiologist or a psychologist. I am a human rights activist, a theologian, a believer in the divine things of God.

If you ask me what my denomination is, I would have to ask you what Jesus' was, or Paul's or Peter's, Mary's, or the Canaanite woman's, and I'm that. I am also a preacher, filmmaker, kite runner, scuba diver, and lover of people; and I know that I would have traded it all for the love of family.

On this journey to heal, I began again, and in the process I fell in love with what the mind could and can do. Oddly enough, before my life took a turn, as a child I was a lover of creation, of how the world came to be and how our own creativity with God's help can be used to build wealth in order to provide for others, community, businesses, and so much more.

When we are trained up by a life of chaos, we often become chaotic in many ways. But when God comes into our lives, when the Lord allows the person of the Holy Spirit to dwell with us, in us, to teach us all things as we receive Him, then we begin to live as His child on deeper levels. The Scriptures say those who are,

"…led by the Spirit of God are the sons God."

Romans 8:14

Thus, He trains us up again. We are His "little children." The wonderful truth in this for me is that, because I was so empty from all of the abuse and all of the mistakes I made trying to live, I realized that unless I was empty, I could not be filled. Unless, as I said earlier, we come like a little child, we cannot enter the kingdom of heaven.

What is so fantastic is that God is the Master Builder. He is the great and only true Architect, and when He builds us up again, we are then a masterpiece. His very own masterpiece. King David wrote:

> **"I will praise thee, for I am fearfully *and* wonderfully made: marvelous *are* thy works; and *that* my soul knoweth right well."**

Psalms 139:14 (KJV)

Praise Corner

Hallelujah! I sing, Hallelujah! I scream aloud, enough so that all can hear that He is Love. When we have His love, we already have everything, and so everything else underneath Your love oh God must chase us down. Your love is at the very top of the heap! Every need, every God-willed prayer, every provision for us, every healing request must find us, chase us, and fulfill its submission to the God of truth. Amen!

"Self-sufficiency is the enemy of salvation. If you are self-sufficient, you have no need of God.

If you have no need of God,
you do not seek Him.
If you do not seek Him, you will not find Him."
William Nicholson, Author

David is praising God in Psalm 139, because he knows, after all he has gone through, how well-constructed and formed he is in the Master's hands. Even with the errors that occur, God's mercy is there. It is good to know that we are fearfully (*fearfully* meaning a reverence for God, an honor for the Lord, in knowing that we cannot live, nor do we desire to live, without Him. We also have come to know in profound divine wisdom that life is not truly possible without Him, nor can it be) and wonderfully made and that we celebrate who we are in Him! His,

"joy is our strength, after all."

Nehemiah 8:10

Let me tell you something: When you have discovered you really know you are loved, you will jump up and down with praise like there is no tomorrow, because His joy is that big. For those who do not know Him but live by His mercy, when you discover more of who you are before you get to know Him, it will lead you that much closer. In a relationship with the Savior, when times get rough, you will,

"have a peace which passeth all understanding,"

Philippians 4:7 (KJV)

One of my favorite sermons or messages was in discovering the paradigm shift that relates to how we see or view something at different times.[1]

Scientist Thomas Kuhn used the duck-rabbit optical

illusion above from the book, The Structure of Scientific Revolutions (1962), to demonstrate the way in which a paradigm shift could cause one to see the same information in an entirely different way.

Kuhn wrote that the subject of a *gestalt* demonstration knows that his perception has shifted because he can make it shift back and forth repeatedly while he holds the same book or piece of paper in his hands.

Aware that nothing in his environment has changed, he directs his attention increasingly not to the figure (duck or rabbit) but to the lines of the paper he is looking at."[2]

This became my life, learning how to learn again. How to view myself through God's eyes and not by what I saw, or thought I saw, in my life. Because Scriptures say:

> **"Be transformed by the renewing of your mind, that you may prove what is the will of God"**

Romans 12:2 (KJV)

Transformation is real, and there is often a scientific process that explains the supernatural.

Like T.D. Jakes in his message on the paradigm shift, as well as Dr. Beverly Bam Crawford, who gave me a biblical and scientific knowledge that explained the mind when I first started my studies, I would search for the scientific properties that God has given us to explain certain things.

All these gifts are a gift of God as the Master Creator! Earlier, we spoke of Dr. Caroline Leaf and her wonderful work on neuroplasticity in the study of neuroscience, the brain's incredible ability to be rewired and to reorganize itself by forming new neural connections and pathways throughout our lives.

There is also the work of Dr. Rebecca Campbell, a psychologist I admire, who studies the brain. One thing that she shared at a symposium I attended (in addition I have studied her PowerPoint papers and other work found at the National Institute of Justice) is what happens to victims under great stress.

Under pressure, the autonomic nervous system creates a *fight or flight* response. Dr. Campbell, however, also explained the process *to freeze*. Freezing interested me because when victims freeze (which is also called *tonic-immobility* or *rape-induced paralysis*), it happens on its own.

Because of this and the discrimination of others, we have a hard time receiving God's Grace in a chaotic world.

Doctors say that tonic immobility happens in up to 50 percent of rape cases. It happens at a higher percentage if the victim has experienced prior sexual trauma.[3] Law enforcement personnel, laypersons, and others wonder why girls, women, and children in trafficking go back and stay in these evil environments.

Well, we know sometimes that it is because, as the heart and mind are formed in this abuse, victims are repeatedly told this life is the only place for them, and that leaving will also get them or someone they love killed. There are many dynamics that create the confusion of why some victims appear to stop fighting, or go back to the abuse. "Stockholm syndrome, or capture-bonding, is a psychological phenomenon in which hostages express empathy and sympathy and have positive feelings toward their captors, sometimes to the point of defending them."[4]

This is only one answer among many. But for me, personally, there was so much happening to my mind that everything became very bizarre.

Rape paralysis occurs in up to 50 percent of first-time rapes, but I think that this is higher with repeated rapes, which create major chaos. Victims of sex-slavery suffer repeated rape, but at some point they have to try and survive.

Therefore, once they arise from that frozen state of some level of tonic immobility or rape paralysis, a victim of sex slavery has to fight to live, and that means often denying reality.

That's what I did, and I think it creates even another set of issues, including various forms of mental and emotional anguish—especially when the trafficker rapes the victim and he or she has to pretend to like it.

In addition, and according to Dr. Campbell, the drugs and alcohol often involved make everything much worse than it already is. And sometimes, this includes a child that a victim was allowed to have in the brothel.

Science also has determined that our minds are formed by our environment; thus, in these severe abuses, the minds have been manipulated to an altered state that is not a true self.

Because of the freezing paralysis and the chemicals and thought processes that are distorted in moments of extreme trauma, the thoughts of what is happening at the time of the attack are filed in various parts of the brain.

In my personal opinion, being perpetually raped (over and over in that moment, that day, and over time) can cause victims to confuse reality with pain, pain with reality, and their true selves with the victims they've become. The former life is buried in a heap, an internal storm, which, over time, creates and rewires who they are, compared with who they were. The repeated paralysis causes victims to be chemically and biologically altered. (What I mean is that I often felt high, lost, and confused in general because of the chemical imbalance created by abuse.) Added to the drugs and quantities of hard alcohol (not wine but *intense* abuse of liquor in strong doses) they are often made to consume these imbalances produce such an altered state of reality that when the people escape that life, they really don't know who they are. And sometimes they don't know that they don't know.

The perpetual rape that they must acquiesce to in order to save their lives causes them to freeze up in other ways. This is what I can see in my own life, then and afterward!

It's like I was walking around but in a catatonic state. Yet, I had become very equipped to do this. I began to form a personality through abuse and lose the total self and the innate reality that God ordained for me to have. It was like I was missing an arm or a leg, for instance, but no one could tell because the prosthetic one was so state-of-the-art, no one even noticed!

This is done so slowly that no one on the outside except the trafficker notices. The trafficker knows this in theory, because that is their purpose and plan all along, but it is much more evil *and* scientific than even they understand.

When I tried to recall, as do many victims, all that had happened from day to day, I became exhausted. I could not read between the lines anymore of who was at fault all of the time and who organized everything that took place every day.

The body and the flesh react when children are raped. Even 18-year-old males in prison who are raped often ejaculate, yet they know they are not homosexual, were fighting it all of the time, and hated it. They know they hated it, but the flesh didn't, meaning the unconscious flesh responded over time, but the conscious heart and mind were fighting.

Young female victims hate it and know they do, but sometimes the flesh will still climax and respond unconsciously with a reflex. This can create self-loathing and confusion as well in an adolescent, as it did in me. Over time it all becomes sickening and horrible.

There are, however, moments in which the victims have to relax and go under the influence to save their lives. And there are times when the trafficker is in the room watching, and the victims can be beaten up if they don't act like they're enjoying the rape.

After a time—a short time, at that, a month or so of repeated rape and seasoning—they think it's their fault. No one has come to the rescue, so it must be.

Even some of the children and girls (five and up) I've mentored who have been raped by their natural fathers, relatives, or stepfathers, think exactly the same thing: that it is their fault. This is crazy!

After a while, a victim doesn't run and doesn't know why not. They don't remember anymore how scared they are.
They forget or don't know that they have been brainwashed and immobilized, and no one else in their world does, either. There is always fear, of everything, but they must downplay that. This is why I call it *soul assassination.* This is the Isaiah 42:22 Scripture that I shared with you, locked in houses of bondage, physically and mentally, and no one says, "Be restored."

> **But this is a people robbed and spoiled; they are all of them snared in holes, and they are hid in prison houses: they are for a prey, and none delivereth; for a spoil, and none said, Restore.**
>
> **Isaiah 42:22**

It's so important to have advocates in the police station and in first-response situations, as well as in anti-trafficking organizations, churches, and other areas. People must know how to ask the right questions, because human-trafficking victims/survivors are purposely altered and brainwashed so that they forget who they are when an officer or person who can help is present.

There are situations in which victims are always trying to escape, and will, but there are also mental anguish, identity issues, and desires that must be dealt with. These are too gruesome and difficult for most survivors to share. When they snap out of it, they have to eat, they have to stay alive, and even then many tend to go through the motions, like people do in life in general.

After months or years of this, what do you think happens? As I said and must say again, if drugs or alcohol are taken, it is even worse, and most traffickers keep victims high. As a result, each time is easier for the traffickers (pimps, johns, tricks, pedophiles) to have their way. Chemical and hormonal processes in the body, as well as psychological ones, are occurring. Thus, they stay and live in the hellholes until other, what I call *life-giving, triggers* scream to fight harder or flee by any means necessary, if they can.

This can be dangerous, because if someone is killed, how does the victim explain? This is what happened in the case of Ruby McCollum.

> "On Sunday morning, August 3, 1952, McCollum shot and killed prominent Live Oak, Florida physician and state senator-elect, Dr. C. Leroy Adams. She accused him of forcing her to submit to sex and bear his child. The case received coverage in both the white and black press, and was instrumental in changing attitudes about the practice of 'paramour rights,' the presumed right of a white man to take a black woman to whom he was not married as his concubine."[5]

Rape is a major crime in America; one in four girls or women (or more) will be raped, as I mentioned earlier. That is 25 to 30 percent of females. Men and boys are raped as well, often in prison; what is extremely hard to bear in mind as well are the young men 17 and up who end up in prison and are repeatedly raped and sodomized. Coming out of prison, who do they open up to? Who do they have to share their anger and pain with before that anger, pain, and bitterness eats away at them?

For men it really is often while incarcerated, and they never talk about it because the guilt of being incarcerated is already overwhelming. And, once again, they too feel it's their fault. This crime is not gender specific, but of course it occurs in far more females than males, with most perpetrators being male. Even when they are out as victims/survivors who become survivors that are thrivers, the road there is not easy and takes time.

Victims must cast down certain thoughts and must be equipped in God to be able to do this, along with therapy and having contact with loved ones. They may even look okay in college, fighting the good fight, but that doesn't mean they are not still hurting.

The Book of Joel speaks about the last days and some of the evil that we must be in intercessory prayer about when fighting for the rights of victims:

> **"And they have cast lots for My people, and have given a boy for a harlot and have sold a girl for juice [of the grape] and have drunk it."**
>
> **Joel 3:3**

Praise God for His Love and guidance through all of this. Even in Zechariah, the Lord speaks about people not hearing. They turn their hearts off so they do not have to deal with the truth, so they do not have to do anything about it. Look at this with me:

> **"And when you ate and when you drank, did you not eat for yourselves and drink for yourselves? Should you not hear the words which the Lord cried by the former prophets when Jerusalem was**

inhabited and in prosperity with her cities round about her, and the South and the plain. But they refused to hearken, and pulled away the shoulder, and stopped their ears, that they should not hear."

Zechariah 7:6-7, 11 (KJV)

Read the entire chapter and you may discover as I did that we are not to close our hearts to the true injustice done to others. That is what is so great about faith; we don't have to do anything alone, and we shouldn't.

We can work on these things together and give the burdens of them all to the Lord.

The same Scriptures even speak on our fasting and whether it is truly for God in love. Look at this with me from verse five of the same book:

"Speak to all the people of the land and to the priests, saying, 'When you fasted and mourned in the fifth and seventh months, even those seventy years you were in exile, was it for Me that you fasted, for Me?'"

Zechariah 7:5

When we close our ears to the truth all around us, we close our eyes and thus our hearts. How can we have faith to hear what to do if we are not open to the depths of the truth of the ills of the flesh and the joy of our salvation through it all? God says that,

"faith comes by hearing and hearing by the Words of God."

Romans 10:17 (KJV)

"What we are reluctant to touch often seems the very fabric of our salvation."

Don DeLillo
Essayist, Novelist, Playwright

All we need to do is lay it all up to the reflection of the light of the glorious Gospel and see what God has to say about the matter.

The Lord says that even the feet of those who carry this good news are beautiful! How beautiful are your feet, Beloved?

His love is like walking on earth yet being prepared to tread on roads paved with gold. This life is hopefully 120 years (Genesis 6:3), and during it all, regardless of how long we are here, it is for the giving of the love given to us by God. No, we didn't always get it, it's true, but that is why He came, isn't it?

> **"And the LORD said, My spirit shall not always strive with man, for that he also is flesh: yet his days shall be an hundred and twenty years"**
>
> **Genesis 6:3 (KJV)**

Now, there is debate related to the Psalms because some versions state 70-80 years, but I know of and have met too many people who live longer.

I think that with fewer toxins, a life of prayer, low stress and anger, and eating food that is *food*, (no soda, no white flour, no white sugar, no processed foods, *and* nothing genetically altered) we can get there. Anyway, that advice was a gift, but in my next workbook and companion to this one, I will go into key things I have done that relate to nutrition, exercise, and rest.

THERE IS MORE THAN HOPE IN LEARNING

Dr. Campbell, whom I greatly admire, described a case that opened my eyes even more. It was about a young lady who was at an "All-American" college frat party. She and a guy who had been drinking wanted to kiss, so they did. In one of the back rooms they fooled around. Many young ladies are really looking for love, not intercourse, and never rape. He started to get really rough, and she began to tell him, "No, no!" He then stuck his elbow on her neck and shoulder, and she said, "No, no, no!" She was in utter shock, but he didn't listen. He raped her. After he was finished raping her, he saw that she was not moving, so under the influence of alcohol and stupidity, he left the room, bragging that he had sex with her and that "She is still lying there." So, several guys went in and proceed to *gang rape* her, one by one. After all of the craziness, her girlfriend overheard, entered the room, and saw her friend. She reacted, grabbed her, and got her out of there.

Later, she described her friend who was being raped as seemingly "dead," as in not there, not moving, heavy. This is the rape-induced paralysis, which Dr. Campbell so powerfully teaches about.

The rape was reported to the police, but because she was just lying there and had been drinking, the officer assumed she wanted it and persuaded her against taking this case any further.

What is so exciting about Dr. Campbell's work is that she also describes the body's chemical makeup under stress and how it affects memory.

In addition, she gives examples of how a person who is not a professional neurobiologist or psychologist who studies this, or a law officer who has been made to take basic courses that give that person informed resources and skills, might not be able to understand some of this behavior.

The officer in the above case was also making assumptions based on the victim's fogginess and lack of clarity, and assumed that because of this, she was lying.

Here is a quote from Dr. Campbell, as I told her I would share some of her work in my book. I spoke a little about the hippocampus earlier and promised to finish. As Dr. Campbell explained:

"When stress hormones are released at such high levels, they are going to impair the hippocampus.

It's going to be difficult for the brain to encode and consolidate this information. So the memories are going to be fragmented when they're stored in the victim's brain. And that means that the recall of this is going to be very slow and difficult."

I often speak about the brain and heart connection in many Scriptures.

As I have said before, in the Bible, the word for *mind* is the same word for *heart*. Here are just a few examples:

> **"Then he said to me, Fear not, Daniel, for from the first day that you set your mind *and* heart to understand and to humble yourself before your God, your words were heard, and I have come as a consequence of [and in response to]."**
>
> **Daniel 10:12**

> **"He has blinded their eyes and hardened *and* benumbed their [callous, degenerated] hearts [He has made their minds dull], to keep them from seeing with their eyes and understanding with their hearts *and* minds and repenting *and* turning to Me to heal them."**
>
> **John 12:40**

> **"For who has known *or* understood the mind (the counsels and purposes) of the Lord so as to guide**

***and* instruct Him *and* give Him knowledge? But we have the mind of Christ (the Messiah) *and* do hold the thoughts (feelings and purposes) of His heart."**

1 Corinthians 2:16

"Pharaoh sent to find out, and behold, there was not one of the cattle of the Israelites dead. But the heart of Pharaoh was hardened [his mind was set] and he did not let the people go."

Exodus 9:7

"Only take heed, and guard your life diligently, lest you forget the things which your eyes have seen and lest they depart from your [mind and] heart all the days of your life. Teach them to your children and your children's children"

Deuteronomy 4:9

"Oh, that they had such a [mind and] heart in them always [reverently] to fear Me and keep all My commandments, that it might go well with them and with their children forever!"

Deuteronomy 5:29

The above Scriptures are biblical experiences that delineate and give not only credence to spiritual purpose of the mind and heart but also validation to more scientific understanding of each organ.

The hippocampus is the structure in the brain that processes information into memories and emotions. It is like a mini-heart and the heart is, in fact, like a smaller brain. I believe that herein lays the subconscious mind. I say all this because this has been my life, from death to life, and it is utterly exhilarating to be able to explain my own awakening in a form that is palatable and, I pray, palpable.

For others who have been abused, whether in these horrific ways or in any way, to realize this, I believe it is crucial to know that you *can* "teach an old dog new tricks." I know how crossed and confused my mind used to feel and how difficult it was to pull it together, how much fear there was. Now, with my hormones popping all over like they do for women 38 and up, all of this is amazing because I eat well, exercise, and take tremendous care to feed myself truth. So, how do we get to this, and why do I believe that in the process of memory the subconscious mind is at the center of the heart? Because it is clear in the Scriptures and in science that this is simply the case.

This is why intense negative emotions due to traumatic experiences, especially those that start at an early age, can cause various disorders, including mental illness. These can present themselves in very minor or very major ways. I know this because I've experienced the minor ones firsthand. It all depends on who we are. A minor thing to one person could be major for another. But in all of this, the amazing irony and even beauty of creation is that God said

> **"There hath no temptation taken you but such as is common to man: but God is faithful, who will not suffer you to be tempted above that ye are able; but will with the temptation also make a way to escape, that ye may be able to bear it."**
>
> **1 Corinthians 10:13 (KJV)**

As I explained before, I was very nervous, suicidal, depressed, and uncomfortable in my own skin, afraid to be around too many people without being high. I was already born with sensitivity, which is a gift, but when distorted by child abuse, it can create problems. Troubled, fatherless, withdrawn, and other characteristics are traits that traffickers/predators and abusers look for in children and adolescents. That is why we have to work through trauma to discover our true self and why one of my favorite Scriptures is

"As a man thinketh in his heart so is he."

Proverbs 23:7 (KJV)

This was exciting to me as a believer on a healing journey to fight for what God has given me. For years, I tried to understand why I hated myself. Why I sabotaged my successes. Why I pushed people away. Why I was afraid to give all of my heart in a relationship. Why I was basically miserable. Why I assumed that I could be okay eventually, but happy, no, not so much, not me, not really. I thought I would settle on "just okay." But that is not why God sent His Son for me and you, to simply settle on just okay. His Word says that we should have fullness of joy! That we should have "exceedingly, abundantly, above all that we ask or think." (Ephesians 3:20)

Well, if 70 percent of communication is nonverbal, then what had I been asking? If this includes what I think, then what have I been thinking?

I had to change it all, a paradigm shift on greater levels than even I understood.

Prayer Corner

Dearest Lord, our God, we pray in earnest. I pray for the reader of this book. My heart cries out to someone that may

be reading this who doesn't fully know who they are and how amazingly wonderful You see them. That Your love has power to wash away every sin done to us and every sin we have committed. That Your love has the power and is waiting to rewire and transform their hearts and minds to be all that You have declared and decreed for them before the foundation of the world. Lord, Jesus, thank You for Your mercy and Grace over their lives right now. Every need that is rooted in Your direction and in the excellence of which you have called them I pray it released right now! I pray for supernatural healing from rape, abuse, molestation, abandonment, loneliness, incest and fear! I speak to the realm of the evil one and boldly declare Lord, that the evil one must depart in the name of Jesus. To the enemy, your work is over here and your stumbling block removed. Your shackles of pain and illness must come off of these people today, right now, in the mighty name of Jesus Christ of Nazareth! Father, we thank You for the healing power, and pray that the very same power that raised up Jesus from the dead will touch the lives of Your child. We thank You for minds being renewed, relationships being mended, marriages being saved! We pray for the married couples that are having intimacy issues because of former abuse to be delivered by Your loving hand today, God, according to your Word in Isaiah, that says that they are healed! Your Word in 1st Peter 2:24, that says they *were* healed! You are the Healer and the Way-maker, Father. Amen and amen.

While I was searching, God was transforming and renewing my mind in this process and I asked and He gave me these Scriptures:

> **"What is the use (profit), my brethren, for anyone to profess to have faith if he has no [good] works**

> **[to show for it]? Can [such] faith save [his soul]? If a brother or sister is poorly clad and lacks food for each day, And one of you says to him, Good-bye! Keep [yourself] warm and well fed, without giving him the necessities for the body, what good does that do. So also faith, if it does not have works (deeds and actions of obedience to back it up), by itself is destitute of power (inoperative, dead)."**
>
> **James 2:14-17**

I began to dig even more into the Scriptures and to supplement them with books and readings from people like Joyce Meyer, Katheryn Kuhlman, T.D. Jakes, Smith Wigglesworth, Robert Morris, Billy Graham, Martin Luther King, Jr., Martin Luther, and many great scientists, poets, health practitioners, and rabbis. The Scriptures were my magnifying glass.

The development of our brains and hearts is key to who a child becomes, who we become.

Rudolph Tanzi, Ph.D., is a neurogeneticist at Harvard University who specializes in Alzheimer's research. He says, "most people simply allow their everyday brain, or 'baseline brain,'" he calls it, "to work unconsciously."[6] However, key areas of the brain involved with memory and learning continue to produce new nerve cells every day. There are three areas of the brain: emotional, instinctive, and intellectual. According to Dr. Tanzi, science and body truth in general is that "we are not our brain." With the study of neuroplasticity, we have the ability to literally change it.

We have the ability to rise above our thoughts, or the thoughts in our minds, observe them, and get rid of the ones that are out of order, the ones that create "dis-order" or disorders.

These negative, destructive thoughts cause stress, anxiety, depression, and other forms of emotional and mental anguish. I have learned to eliminate these disordered thoughts, and over time with other therapy and support and my life in God, this change has brought profound healing and new life.

This is what it means when Scripture says:

> **"Casting down imaginations, and every high thing that exalteth itself against the knowledge of God, and bringing into captivity every thought to the obedience of Christ."**
>
> **2 Corinthians 10:5 (KJV)**

We are spirit. We have a soul. We live in a body. What this means is that our soul is in the middle of our spirit and our mind. Thus, how are we to hear clearly from God when it is all broken up? How are we to maneuver in this world when our soul is broken?

Music brings a healing peace, as it did when David played for troubled King Saul. Music and even reading the Word is in sympathy with all three parts of the brain—it is emotional, intellectual, and instinctive at the same time. Thus, it brings a calming and healing effect.

This is the importance of studying the Word of God, as the Scriptures are,

> **"spirit and they are life."**
>
> **John 6:63 (KJV)**

They help balance the functions of the brain and, thus, the heart. Worship and soft praise music are also soothing to the soul, in addition to meditation.

It is good to go to a quiet place, as the Lord did, and to commune quietly with Him, as He did with the Father. It is good to rest and spend this "power time" with the Holy Spirit to hear and be comforted and refreshed, being made whole and healed on a perpetual level as we live.

KNOWING THIS WAS THE KEY FOR ME

I wrote earlier that one of my favorite messages involved discovering the paradigm shift as related to how we see or view something at different times.[7]

You see, simply because we have thoughts that are on our minds all day long does not mean that those thoughts are ours.

Whether they are or not, it still doesn't mean we have to entertain them. Even in therapy, I had to affirm things in speech, in thoughts, and in writing. My first therapist, who was not a believer, still operated in the realm of the psychological profession, which describes, in part, the divine workings of how the body heals. The opposite is true, as unforgivingness, stress, and hatred cause physical and mental sickness. So what did I do?

> **"Finally, brethren, whatsoever things are true, whatsoever things are honest, whatsoever things are just, whatsoever things are pure, whatsoever things are lovely, whatsoever things are of good report; if there be any virtue, and if there be any praise, think on these things."**
>
> **Philippians 4:8 (KJV)**

I began to think and speak what I longed for. In speaking and applying what God says about who I am, even when I wasn't fully sure, I began to heal all the more. The Bible says the tongue is like *the rudder of a ship.* That is amazing as well because I love boats and the ocean, and rudders are so very small, as Scriptures say, yet they guide this enormous vessel. We are also a vessel, and with the power of God's love, with the Holy Spirit at the helm, we cannot fail.

> **"What? know ye not that your body is the temple of the Holy Ghost which is in you, which ye have of God, and ye are not your own? For ye are bought with a price: therefore glorify God in your body, and in your spirit, which are God's."**
>
> **1 Corinthians 6:19-20 (KJV)**

We are not our own. This means we are not *on* our own, and that is good news to me, because I can barely tie a shoelace without the Lord or, let's just say, I don't want to. But God the Father and the Son by the Holy Spirit has given us ways of escape, to be survivors and thrivers, no longer victims tossed to and fro.

> **"For though we walk in the flesh, we do not war after the flesh: (For the weapons of our warfare are not carnal, but mighty through God to the pulling down of strong holds;) Casting down imaginations, and every high thing that exalteth itself against the knowledge of God, and bringing into captivity every thought to the obedience of Christ."**
>
> **2 Corinthians 10:3-5 (KJV)**

The King James Version of the Bible says our weapons are "mighty." So our spirit works with our soul to cast down and bring these thoughts into the submission of truth—the truth of who we really are and who we were born to be, regardless of what has happened. I don't care if the bondage that has harmed you has nothing to do with trafficking, domestic violence, or rape, because these issues in life are the revealed secrets of a greater bondage in the world and in the hearts of human beings, saved and unsaved.

This book was written in the hope that many will find and discover freedom from all forms of bondage, even those that we cause ourselves. We are transformed by the renewing of our mind so that we can, like Scripture says,

"prove what is the will of God."

Romans 12:2 (KJV)

This is for our own lives. His will in effect deals with His will for our lives. This means what we do, where we go, how we live, what our gifts are, what our life's work and purpose looks like, and how it will affect others in knowing who He really is. We don't get to the mountaintop to say "Look at me," but rather, "Look at who brought me here to be able to see more clearly where I need to be and how I'm going to get there."

God, who is rich in mercy, can deliver us out of all forms of bondage! You have time to do only that which you were born to do, and if you do not do that, you will not be at rest. In an interview for *Ebony* magazine, journalist Michelle Buford asked me, "When did you get out of child sex slavery, Brook?" My response was, "I've spent my whole life getting out." It has been the process of awakening that I call the "Helen Keller process." Helen Keller was born able to see and hear until she was approximately one and a half years old. But something happened. She then became very sick with, "an acute congestion of the stomach and brain."

According to Wikipedia, "in 1886, when Keller was six years old, her mother read Charles Dickens' *American Notes*, which were accounts of his travels through North America in 1842. The particular bit of those writings that intrigued her was a part about a deaf-blind woman that was successfully educated, something she had previously thought wouldn't be possible. She then sought to find a teacher for her daughter. Her search eventually led her to famed inventor Alexander Graham Bell, who at the time was a teacher of deaf children (incidentally, his wife and mother were both deaf). Bell recommended Helen's parents to the Perkins Institute for the Blind in South Boston. Once there, a 20-year-old, visually-impaired woman by the name of Anne Sullivan was asked to become Keller's instructor and eventually governess and constant companion. Their relationship lasted in this way for nearly 50 years."[8]

She was an exceptional girl and woman-child. Everyone thought she was deaf, blind, and dumb, with no real balanced emotions; yet she became the first deaf/blind person to earn a Bachelor of Arts degree. She also became a political activist and lecturer. But at one time in her history, they thought her a wild animal. Because she could not communicate normally, she became angry. The negative and judgmental words strangers and others must have spoken over her as they saw this blind and deaf girl in this state carried a vibration of hate, confusion, fear, and God-knows-what. But her teacher, found by her mother, did not give up. They stood in the gap and interceded for her.

Oddly enough, it did not seem for a long time like anything was getting through to Helen until one day, all that was placed in her heart and mind clicked! The love, the hugs she could feel, the vibration of them just clicked! She went from mouthing nothing anyone understood, and making few symbols, to understanding and communicating all that was around her—all that was taught her by this precious teacher. Something horrible happened that changed her life, and something as wonderful helped her transform past it!

Now, if someone did not give up on one of God's beloved who could neither see nor hear, how do we give up on those that can? How can we give up on each other? Why have we given up on victims of human trafficking or other abuses when all they need is God in us?

Just like Helen Keller, who one day spoke, "Apple!" I said, "I'm Free," and so can you!

I get it, I see it, Lord: your love, my life. I see, I was once blinded for so many reasons, and now, I see! And so I forgave and forgave again, and the rest is history, or I could say her-story.

It's good to stand in the gap for others. And alongside us, our God. Our heavenly Father says this,

> **"And I sought for a man among them that should make up the hedge, and stand in the gap before me for the land, that I should not destroy it: but I found none."**
>
> **Ezekiel 22:30 (KJV)**

WHAT ARE SOME OF THE OTHER ISSUES THAT ABUSED CHILDREN DEAL WITH AND WHAT ARE SOME OF THE CAUSES?

According to Dr. James Mercy, there are "extreme high stresses that children in trafficking deal with."[9] I realize this, but I also know that as the child grows up, it's the same without help, and even worse. These crimes have caused disorders such as schizophrenia, bipolar disorder, and PTSD. Many victims of it complain they have thoughts of suicide, anxiety, lack of feelings, self-hatred, mental confusion, low self-esteem, drug addiction, and trust issues. Some even become pedophiles. Some abused children are so angry that they get involved in a number of crimes, including serious gang warfare, aiding and abetting criminals, burglary, extreme violence, murder, and rape.

Dr. Mercy also goes on to say that "family background, harsh and inconsistent parenting, physical and emotional maltreatment, sexual abuse, parental alcohol abuse, parental incarceration, witnessing abuse in the home,"[10] create isolation and grave issues in children.

Dr. Mercy's work also discusses the fact that when a child is exposed to abuse, it has a predictably negative impact in shaping who they become. The interaction we human beings experience, whether good or bad, has an awesome effect on our brains. Because of all of the exposures I have experienced, I should be "lost in translation," and I was, to some degree, but thank God for His mercy. We also are able to hide our pain all too well or find escape in sex, drugs, and everything else, except God, who helps us to cope with the pain.

MORE WAYS I TURNED IT AROUND

> **"This Book of the Law shall not depart out of your mouth, but you shall meditate on it day and night, that you may observe *and* do according to all that is written in it. For then you shall make your way prosperous, and then you shall deal wisely *and* have good success."**
>
> **Joshua 1:8**

I began to understand that my heart needed to be guarded, but not the way I thought. Important was not only what I let in but also what I meditated on and what I allowed to remain. I had to guard my heart from myself and trust God in all things. The Bible says,

> **"guard your heart for out of it flows the issues of life."**
>
> **Proverbs 4:23 (KJV)**

We often think that when we are guarding our hearts, it's from other people and things on the outside, but one of the words for *guard* in Greek means *to search within.* Therefore, that's what I did.

IT'S A LIFE-LONG PROCESS

> **"But I say to you that everyone who looks at a woman with lustful intent has already committed adultery with her in his heart."**
>
> **Matthew 5:28**

When memories are formed, they travel through the hippocampus, which organizes them and sends them off for storage in the cerebral cortex. This creates who we are in many ways, when they become a part of our long-term memory. When they are short-term memories and we have to recall them to describe who we are, or when describing our traumatic experience as a victim of rape or other violence to a first responder, our parents, a friend, or whomever, it is going to be difficult.

Long-term memories are different and when associated with strong emotions are just that—stronger and easier to recall. This is why we remember bad emotional memories and happy emotional memories most easily. For this reason it is so very important how we approach, speak to, and hear young adults, children, and one another all around us. Another key ingredient in healing and preventing a child from being hurt, whether from the outside or from within, is *listening.*

It is amazing how some think this is simple, but statistics show that it is the hardest thing for many to accomplish.

I would often try and tell my story, and as soon as someone seemed slightly intrigued, I'd test a little further and find myself stopping, because most did not take the time to lean in and listen.

I can remember a time when I went to speak to one of my counselors. I found someone who loved God, and I thought, "Great!" But without any understanding of what takes place with sexual abuse or child sex slavery, the therapist began to speak about the fact that something was wrong with me and would be for a long time before I could unravel it for therapy or for myself.

This happened at church! At that time I didn't realize that

many counselors in the church setting are not equipped for dealing with severe abuse. Yet they sometimes try to handle it without stating that, yes, it is a spiritual matter but it is also a scientifically validated psychological one, and they realize and admit that they are not equipped to handle it alone.

It is appropriate and often necessary to refer parishioners to trusted professionals; we often need both faith and psychological counsel.

I started working out at Bally's at that time, and I had an agent and was on my way, so to speak, in theatre and film. At the same time, at SRF fellowship I began doing a six-month course on meditation. My focus was Jesus and a few Scriptures from the Bible that were in the book written by Paramahansa. These generally were, "I will meditate on thy Word day and night." For 45 minutes in the morning and another 45 in the evening, I would start the meditation process by breathing deeply to relax my thoughts and clear out all of the noise. Then I would softly sing a worship song and pray for my family, friends, and destiny in every aspect of my life and theirs, along with praying for right decision-making and good friends. After that, I would remain quiet and softly sing in a whisper or breathe a word of thanks every few minutes, or simply rest, listen, be still, and know that God is God. I would ask the Lord to speak, to show me the way.

This became very powerful, and the time seemed to pass so quickly that it became easy to sit still. I should say that normally that was not easy for me. I cannot remember previously sitting still for long as an adult; perhaps, as a young girl lying down looking at the sky, I could. But in my later years, it was no easy task.

One day I had been praying to the Lord and asking Him about salvation, guidance, and the purpose of life. Suddenly, it was as if the ceiling had opened up, along with my mind, and a cool breeze blew in and swept through my body. It felt as if my whole body was filled with a shock of some kind and was tingling from head to toe. I then started singing; at the time, I thought it was in

African, I didn't *know* what it was, but I was singing in the Spirit, in the gift of tongues, before I knew what they were.

"He who speaks in a [strange] tongue edifies *and* improves himself, but he who prophesies [interpreting the divine will and purpose and teaching with inspiration] edifies *and* improves the church *and* promotes growth [in Christian wisdom, piety, holiness, and happiness]. Then what am I to do? I will pray with my spirit [by the Holy Spirit that is within me], but I will also pray [intelligently] with my mind *and* understanding; I will sing with my spirit [by the Holy Spirit that is within me], but I will sing [intelligently] with my mind *and* understanding also."

1 Corinthians 14:4,15

God is great! Because I needed all of this. In the last several months before I was "born from above," I had met a man named Rudy at the gym.

He was very kind; he would say a friendly hello, and would always ask me if I was okay and doing well in my work as an actor. I had already booked my first few national commercials; I had done my first major film, "The Silencer," in the nineties and gotten my SAG card (Screen Actors Guild), which is granted only when a production/producer uses the Taft Hartly Act to indicate that, out of the thousands of those who are already members of SAG, I, a one member at the time was, to the production team, the best person for the role. This is a great moment for any actor. (The other way to be a member of SAG is to do a bunch of extra roles and collect vouchers until you reach a certain amount, which can take some time.)

I was still addicted, with many difficult issues, but it was not the same type of hell that I had suffered before. I, like many, thought that this hell was not hell at all. But something began to change, something that would give me the strength to walk alongside God.

Even if delivered, I would have to say "no" to many things, many thoughts, and many behaviors, and I would need assistance to recognize the degree of disorder in which I lived.

Rudy asked me if I went to church. I told him that I was going to SRF and that it was nice.

He never made me feel bad or small; he would always say, "Oh, that's really nice...well...you should come to the church I go to, also. You might like it."

He asked me several times, with so much kindness, and I am sure he was praying for me. So, because he was so gracious, not religious, not pushy, but kind yet persistent, one day I got up and decided to go.

It was after the praying in tongues experience in my room. Between that and the dreams, I thought I was going crazy.

After all, the friends that I had told thought that's what it sounded like to them. I knew it was something special but could not explain it.

The day I woke up to go to church, I had a new feeling and impression in my heart. I was very happy that day. I was also very nervous and suffered a little anxiety, but I made it there from where I lived, near Larchmont Village in the Hancock Park area of Los Angeles, in about 30 minutes. I parked and sat in the car for a bit, just watching people from the church congregation. I walked in and discovered that the pastor of the house Pastor Beverly Bam Crawford, D.D., of Bible Enrichment Fellowship Church International in Inglewood, California, was not there. But her assistant pastor, Pastor Gerald Lee, was preaching the Sunday message that day.

When I walked in, they told me to wait and not to take a seat just yet, because they were in a prayer session of great magnitude. I didn't understand at first, I thought they were being abrupt and rude because I didn't know their protocol. Nor did I have many of the understandings that someone my age could or should have had, had things in my life been different.

The woman at the door wasn't exactly dripping with sweetness. I mean, from the pulpit to the pew is not *always* sweet honey drippings, but I didn't come for that, and guess what? They were speaking it—they were speaking that same kind of language that had happened to me in my room! I had never heard of it outside of these two places. I was flabbergasted, my jaw dropped, like a hungry child in a burger shop or a starving health geek like myself in Whole Foods Market. I was still motionless, and the flutter of God began to speak volumes to me.

I glided to my seat; I wasn't all that smooth, really, but it was the best glide I could manage at the time. I sat in the third row from the front, with about a thousand people. They sat me there, ushered me right up front, of all places. It must have been the "hungry" sign on my forehead.

I sat down and listened and was in such awe! They sang songs that heaven's choir constructed, and I knew I was home. I knew that the Lord was my home. They asked the first-time visitors to stand; that was rough. I stood quickly and eased back down again, but then they said, "No, keep standing." So, I eased back up with a great and mighty fear, shaking in my knees. I took the free gift they handed to me and sat back down. I was mesmerized by the message. I had never heard so many answers to my problems in less than two hours, if ever I could remember. At the end of Pastor Lee's sermon or teaching, he had an altar call for healing, for salvation, for prayer, and to join the church. I went up for salvation, and he led me to the Lord. I have to say, it has not always been an easy ride and to be honest, it became harder after that. But I have never looked back, and pray I never will.

Salvation, I learned, would be about letting go of *all* of it—*everything* that had ever happened and the results of it. Like the abortions that seemed to never leave my mind; was it my fault?

Doctors attest that the grave effects on females who have

abortions include profound grief, depression, and unworthiness, even if not noticed by others. Looking back, I do realize that abortion clinics have a positive opportunity to rescue so many girls and women who become pregnant through rape, various forms of sex slavery, and any form of trafficking. I walked in and out of there unnoticed, and lost. Even that, I had to let go. I always thought I would be a mother, but I had to let go of that dream because my womb was damaged in one or more of the abortions. I do believe in the supernatural power of God, but it is as the Spirit wills. Matthew 10 and 16 display a verse of Scripture that for me was like learning how to free fall into the arms of love. It would be the hardest thing for me to strive to accomplish, but once I did, it would be my greatest gift.

> **"Whoever finds his [lower] life will lose it [the higher life], and whoever loses his [lower] life on My account will find it [the higher life]."**
>
> **Matthew 10:39**

> **"For whoever is bent on saving his [temporal] life [his comfort and security here] shall lose it [eternal life]; and whoever loses his life [his comfort and security here] for My sake shall find it [life everlasting]."**
>
> **Matthew 16:25**

This spoke to me, saying that without God there is no life at all, here or eternally. He is life and loves us so much that Scripture says:

> **"For with You is the fountain of life; in Your light do we see light."**
>
> **Psalms 36:9**

10
LETTING GO

When I'd thought of "letting go" before, they were just words. Words that are read only reflect our ability to understand them in the spirit in which we live. Our understanding of them is based on the deep concept of who we are and what we've experienced, unless we surrender. This is what blocked the truth from me. The Bible speaks about how our conscience plays a role:

> **"Your eye is the lamp of your body; when your eye (your conscience) is sound *and* fulfilling its office, your whole body is full of light; but when it is not sound *and* is not fulfilling its office, your body is full of darkness."**
>
> **Luke 11:34**

What is wonderful is the sense in this Scripture. The word for the "eye being single" has to do with what is in fact behind and above the eyes: the mind. In conscience, "con-science," *con* means to persuade; thus, our mind is persuaded in knowing whether something is right or wrong, positive or negative for us to do or not.

God reveals to us supernaturally by the Holy Spirit that there is something scientific happening in our hearts and minds when we single our minds and thoughts on desired outcomes by not being scatter brained but by being single or clear minded and focused.

This is why, of course, eating a healthy diet is key to overall mental and physical health. As you can see by now, I long for folks to take care of the only bodies we have.

When the science of your mind and heart is muddled with confusion, through acts that the enemy causes to happen to children and adults and those harmful acts that we do to ourselves, it creates disruption in our growth and in hearing from God. This is why being still and resting in Him is crucial to the life of a believer. Science will tell you that prayer and reading Scripture in and out of meditation, and even deep relaxing breaths, help to balance the neurotransmitters—the pathways in the mind.

That does not sound "New Age" to me, it just sounds like biblical wisdom and truth. When we are quiet and healthy, it is easy to hear and sense what our conscience truly believes about a thing.

This is another Scripture about the conscience:

> **"Therefore I always exercise *and* discipline myself [mortifying my body, deadening my carnal affections, bodily appetites, and worldly desires, endeavoring in all respects] to have a clear (unshaken, blameless) conscience, void of offense toward God and toward men."**
>
> **Acts 24:16**

I would finally realize that I was not sound, nor was I fulfilling any office (destiny), whether it was initially my fault or not. My conscience was not clear, and I was always uneasy. If God were as real as I had hoped, it would mean that I would find my life, my soul, and discover my spirit man and the true life God meant for me to have. It would also mean that in faith, if I could achieve His dream for me, which was and is far greater than I could imagine… then what a testimony I could share to His glory.

I've come to realize that because of what took place in the Garden of Eden, I was responsible. I am a part of Adam and Eve; I am human, after all. Thus, I needed the transformative healing power of God in which, through Him, through His love, I can now eat from the "tree of life." My life was not about what I experienced. My life, I would find, was hidden in Christ and would be one of the greatest hidden treasures I would uncover. The treasures that Scriptures speak of—my very own life—would be a hidden treasure that my Lord was waiting to show me! My life, in Him, was now based on my reflection in the eyes of Jesus and not the reflection of my past!

The "it is finished" Savior who died to show me who I really was and could be in a dying world, has shown me the true meaning of life and freedom. All we need to do is see it. The dead eyes of enemies and foes and the ugly past or present that we have faced no longer have power over us, because, according to the Word of God, we will not

"be afraid of their faces."

Jeremiah 1:8

It wasn't all easy, because when you tell the devil who you are, he will pursue trouble for you. But God will deliver us out of them all (2 Timothy 3:11).

***"You have been having our rights so long, that you think, like a slave-holder, that you own us. I know that it is hard for one who has held the reins for so long to give up; it cuts like a knife.
It will feel all the better when it closes up again."***

Sojourner Truth,
Author, Abolitionist, Activist, Former Slave

This profound truth by one of our country's leaders and pioneers of God's love led me to compassion. It reveals the profound and possible ills of the flesh and evil, yet the passion of Christ to heal us and deliver us from every one of them.

I dare say if you have not yet pressed past the junkyard of the past to live above the noise, please do. Be polite and kind to yourself, and dream again and again and again. Realize that your dreams were never created by you, nor were they created for you in the first place. They are gifts of and from God. There are spiritual gifts in the Scriptures, and here is what the Word of God states:

> **"Now there are distinctive varieties *and* distributions of endowments (gifts, extraordinary powers distinguishing certain Christians, due to the power of divine grace operating in their souls by the Holy Spirit) and they vary, but the [Holy] Spirit remains the same. To one is given in *and* through the [Holy] Spirit [the power to speak] a message of wisdom, and to another [the power to express] a word of knowledge *and* understanding according to the same [Holy] Spirit; To another [wonder-working] faith by the same [Holy] Spirit, to another the extraordinary powers of healing by the one Spirit; To another the working of miracles, to another prophetic insight."**
>
> **1 Corinthians 12:4, 8-10**

Ephesians 4:8 deals with the Lord giving gifts unto men as well:

> **"Wherefore he saith, When he ascended up on high, he led captivity captive, and gave gifts unto men"**
>
> **Ephesians 4:8 (KJV)**

Note that verse 11 of Ephesians describes what gifts are:

> **"And he gave some, apostles; and some, prophets; and some, evangelists; and some, pastors and teachers."**
>
> **Ephesians 4:11(KJV)**

Interesting, isn't it? The reason that I stress this is that, when I *began* living free, I discovered an acting career, and became born again, I didn't know what I had accomplished, because I was so broken. There would be nothing that could ever fill me up, no matter how hard I tried. With fervent action, rather, I experienced even more stress over not being where I thought I should be. I also doubted that anything I did would be good enough to cleanse me from the past.

I was so focused on getting more acting jobs, through the talent that I thought was a *gift* that I never had time to heal. The arts helped me with expression, but I exaggerated its importance to myself, as though my career could save me. I would say, "When I have enough funds as an actress, then I will feed millions around the world and save children and women from harm and bring reconciliation from racism."

And, I told myself, "I'll do more, then, when I am clean enough. I will help many people," or "God, look, I need this part or that part because I had all of these plans to build things for others." One day I would heal, and then I could begin to help others heal. I was helping in many ways but not in the way I knew in my heart I was meant to, from birth. Nothing I could accomplish in the arts could wash away the sin done to me or that I had done—nothing, that is, but the precious blood of the Lamb that was slain. This is the *Passover*, this is why we celebrate *Easter* or *Resurrection Sunday*, after all.

Looking back, I often shook off the truth of my own conscience. I worked a lot as an actress and was never satisfied. I never rested in Him. Not until I let go and said, "Lord, not my will but Thy will be done."

I asked for this, in prayer: "Lord, not my will but thy will be done." I was finally able to say this and mean it. When I was able to pray this to God and mean it, then I began to heal all the more. I realized that it was not about me. God is so awesome that the only *true gifts* are the ones mentioned in the Scriptures.

Being an actress, doctor, musician, for example, is not a true gift but an ability. This can be ignited as gifts of a certain kind, but only when given to God. When the Holy Spirit has the free reign to operate in them, *then* they are gifts, because then they are *given* to others through the love of God. They are ignited as gifts when they are given, and illuminate others with joy and new realizations, new thoughts. Thus, they are also being used for kingdom building because they are no longer motivated by self-will, desire, or personal gain. God rewards those who diligently seek Him, and you cannot out-do God's endless generosity; He wouldn't allow it. Our Father is fathomless in His grace and all blessings that He showers on us. Eventually we realize that our gifts are not, nor ever were, ours. People say, "my gift" this and "my gift" that, but it is only when we die that we live. It was only when Christ died that He lived, and we along with Him. He paid the ultimate sacrifice and gave the ultimate gift. Yet it was not fully ignited until He let go of His life to suffer and do the will of the Father.

He sacrificed Himself on the Cross…

> **"Saying, Father, if thou be willing, remove this cup from me: nevertheless not my will, but thine, be done."**
>
> **Luke 22:42 (KJV)**

The Word of God speaks about hidden riches and treasures of darkness being revealed to His beloved children:

> **"And I will give you the treasures of darkness and Hidden riches of secret places, that you may know that it is I, the Lord, the God of Israel, Who calls you by your name."**
>
> **Isaiah 45:3 (KJV)**

According to Scripture, I realized that what the devil does is to try and *destroy* us. Why? Because all was stripped from him; he is wickedly covetous and jealous of what we have and, more importantly, jealous of Jesus our Lord. Some Scriptures deserve to be read again, and the following is no different:

> **"Be sober, be vigilant, because your adversary the devil walketh about as a roaring lion, seeking whom he may devour."**
>
> **1 Peter 5:8 (KJV)**

I began to understand that my greatest treasure outside of knowing who God is, was myself, in Him. The enemy desperately hides this from many, including all of us before Salvation and certain aspects of God, even after receiving Salvation.

One of my greatest treasures was knowing who I was born to be! The hidden riches of life for me were knowing Jesus and, through Him, discovering who I was; my personality, my opinion, destiny, witness, understanding, knowledge, intelligence, abilities, spiritual gifts, my IDENTITY. This was and is my greatest treasure and my richest possession. These are true riches, and I know that this is what we all strive for and what I pray you have. And if you do, then I pray that you have it all the more. There is not a girl, boy, or woman in bondage, on the street, or in houses of bondage who cannot be freed with God's help! We cannot also push people to believe what we believe; we can only love them and give them room enough to hear from God on their own.

Prayer Corner

Dear Lord, may the joy of your unquestionable love and Salvation dwell deeply in the midst of whosoever is holding this book right now as well as those we pray for daily. Father, we pray and declare by the person of the Holy Spirit for the true discovery of who they are on levels that far exceed what they know now. Lord, I pray that it is not a coincidence but a special time of learning, of revelation, of discovery. Lord, I thank you for newness of life and supernatural manifestations of your Grace in operation in their lives as they reach forth to receive all that you have for them and all that you have through them for others. I thank you for the provision of the vision that comes and for the sustenance that is only found in you. Yes, Lord, we shout, "Hallelujah, hallelujah!" to your name, dearest Father, our Lord, Savior, and Redeemer.

Hebrew Prayer: ***Barukh ata Adonai Eloheinu melekh ha-olam shehakol bara lichvodo.*** **(Translation: "Blessed are You, LORD, our God, sovereign of the universe, who created everything for His Glory.")**

Amen.

What do I know now? Having given it all over to the Master's hands, I've discovered that I had to let it all go with head relaxed, to free-fall into His eternal and proven hands, to cast away all blame, and to forgive myself for being too young to understand.

I had to stop wasting another moment of this gift of life, bogged down with what could have been. I had to let go of the years I once felt I missed, not knowing who I was because of the disorders I had suffered. It was imperative that I thank God for right now, this present moment; to let go and celebrate my life.

It's curious. When I left acting for a time, they probably thought of me as a has-been, but I actually feel like a "just now."

I'm just here, now, for the first time, and I can't worry what others think. I have had birthdays in recent years and never wanted to celebrate them because of the shame I felt over not being or accomplishing what I thought I should by this age. But then God freed me from this pain and taught me not to compare my life with others. An orchid cannot be compared to a bird of paradise, a daisy to a rose, or a daffodil to a lily. They are all beautifully fragrant to Him.

As long as my feet can still stretch into the sand and walk along the shores and up mountains of earth and down streets of life, I celebrate this gift of being here for God's purpose. I know that my Redeemer lives! Whether in this life or the one to come, I am forever in His hands.

I just had a birthday while writing this book and, as unpopular as it seems at certain advancing ages these days, I celebrate *all* that it is. I celebrate even though I don't think of age much, compared to the Glory of God and what He desires to accomplish.

I celebrate even though I feel so much younger! Most survivors are late bloomers; we just seem to take more time to wake up from the depths of confusion and identity unfound to breathe with new life again unbound. I am just beginning, and for the first time, I'm unafraid to celebrate and share it with you.

"When someone finds himself quite unjustly attacked and hated on all sides, there is no need for such a person to feel dismayed by misfortune. See how Fortune, who has harmed many a one, is so inconstant, for God, Who opposes all wrong deeds, raises up those in whom hope dwells."

Christine de Pizan
Le **Ditie** de Jehanne d Arc
French Poet and Historian

Let your hope be in the One who cares for you and the only One who has the power to turn your life around!

"Go confidently in the directions of your dreams. Live the life you have imagined."

Henry David Thoreau
Author, Poet, Abolitionist

11

HEARING THE HOLY SPIRIT

"A recent report demonstrated that 8-month-olds can segment a continuous stream of speech syllables, containing no acoustic or prosodic cues to word boundaries, into word like units after only 2 minutes of listening experience."[1]

Saffran, Aslin, & Newport, 1996

You can now see why I cannot live without His presence and how crucial it was for me to receive all of who God is and be baptized in Him as well.

"I have baptized you with water, but he will baptize you with the Holy Spirit."

Mark 1:8

The Holy Spirit is mesmerizing, and even though the lexical reach is large, making it hard to narrow down the vastness of what His name means, it is incredible! I love the Amplified Bible, as well as all the five versions taken from original text.

It is called the Amplified because it expounds on words. No language fully translates to English; so, many times when we say, "What does that mean in English?" we get an answer, but mostly it is only in part. Oftentimes, it is only yes, kind of, sort of, but not the full meaning of expression as if we spoke that language that is foreign to us. So, the lexical reach of a word can mean that one word in Greek or Hebrew can amount to 2 dozen words in English to explain it more fully. And even then, layers and depths of its meaning may be lost.

It is important to know that when we study Scripture without fully knowing ancient Hebrew or Greek, we get parts of the meaning. Often, our words are just not enough to describe the love of God, try as we may. This is why the impressions the Holy Spirit gives us as we read and study the Word are important, because *then* we are sensing and feeling His love and guidance. We know sometimes, when we try and describe something that God did for us, we just "can't find the words." We also need to compare what we hear with Scriptures, and the Holy Spirit will bear witness with our own spirit that we are on the right track.

There are also, in my prayer corner, mentors with whom I share new thoughts and ideas, which have helped me along the way.

The Bible says that the Words of God are "spirit and they are life!"

When we describe the Holy Spirit, we can start briefly with the root word and its meaning. Then we can go to the usage word and the root word for *that*, and its meaning. The word for the Holy Spirit is a noun, of course, *Paraclete*; as I mentioned earlier, it is an advocate or intercessor—the Holy Spirit; the Comforter.

In late Latin, the word is *Paracletus*, and in late Greek, *Parákltos*: comforter, literally (person) called in (to help) who comes alongside us. What the Holy Spirit does, for lack of the fullness of the root word, is to comfort. The root word as described earlier in the book, is *Parakaleo*, which is to call to one's side, call for, summon; to address, speak to, (call upon), which may be done in he way of exhortation, entreaty, comfort, instruction, and so on; to admonish, exhort, to console, to encourage and strengthen by consolation, to comfort, and so on. Beautiful, right? This is what the Holy Spirit does. He:

Entreats: Asks someone (us) earnestly or anxiously to do something.

Appeals: Earnestly requests aid, also, the power or ability to attract.

Begs: Asks (someone) earnestly or humbly for something: "a leper begged Jesus for help"; "she begged me to say nothing to her father."

Beseeches: Asks (someone) urgently and fervently to do something; implore; entreat: "they beseeched him to stay."

Comforts: Imparts a state of physical ease and freedom from pain or constraint.

Conciliates: Stops (someone) from being angry or discontented; placates; pacifies; acts as a mediator.

Preaches: Proclaims, Heralds, and Delivers a sermon; publicly proclaim or teach, encourage; give support, confidence, or hope to (someone): "encouraging results"; give support and advice to (someone) to do or continue something.[2]

He comes alongside us with gentle love and truth. To God, correcting us is done out of love. He also comforts us, for it saves us from mistakes, pain and future destructive situations and choices.

Some at church may call this a "ministry of encouragement," if churches have such departments. This has been one of my greatest gifts and this is what More Too Life is all about: encouraging others to reach out and dream big, to get past all the ills that have happened to them. One of the greatest gifts is from the Holy Spirit (also called the Holy Ghost), being born from above and being baptized with water and the Holy Spirit.

My first memory of hearing Him was through my stepfather, who was Catholic. I was about nine and went to Mass with him. The name of Jesus always stood out to me as a little girl, and I knew it was God calling me somehow; but I didn't really understand the full concept of God. Between you and me, I'm still learning more about Him every day!

In order to try and have closeness with a father, I would go to Mass with my stepfather. I took Holy Communion and was baptized. Of course, I didn't get born again and would not come to know God until much, much later; but in this one year of my life, going to Mass, I heard God speak. I got an impression and a sense that, as bad as things would become, one day He and I would have work to do together. I sensed that somehow, some day, I was to live a life where He would be at the center, and that was that.

Sometimes, I think that's why, when you ask a child what they want to be, they will say, "nurse," "fireman," or "doctor"—because they sense that life is for the *service* of others but cannot explain it. But they intuitively pick from the life-roles they see around them; they choose from what they understand as service.

Sadly, I would not carry those positive thoughts and intuitions very long; too much happened to me, suddenly. But I would remember, even if dimly, "through the noise."

One day, in Hollywood when I was working as an actress, I was walking on Sunset Boulevard, leaving the office of an agent and having a stroll. I hadn't had much time on this side of Sunset. I hadn't been born again, but I did have Holy Communion at nine. I still had not discovered, however, that the Lord was really who He said He was, that all that He said was true, and that He is

"the way, the truth, and the life."

John 14:6

When I was trafficked in L.A., it was near east Sunset, and I hadn't been there for some years. As I walked out of the office, I could hear the Holy Spirit, although I thought it my own voice (and it was and often is). He said to me, "Just take a walk, and go this way." So, this time, I did not argue with the voice, as I often did, because I wanted to do just that; I felt like I needed to walk. As I walked, I could hear Him, but it sounded like me saying, "Look down," so I did. On the sidewalk was a checkbook. It was lying in front of a brown Rolls-Royce or Bentley, one of those. I picked up the checkbook,. looked around, and thought, "Where to go?" I opened up the checkbook and the checks had a name and address. The name was Latoya Jackson. My heart stopped, and I was a little nervous. Then the voice said, "Go into the store." Well, there were many stores in the neighborhood, but one small boutique stood out.

I walked in and out of the corner of my eye, I could see singer and artist Janet Jackson and her sister, Latoya. I started to shake a bit and just wanted to run out of the place in fear, but I didn't. I held up the checkbook, sort of closed my eyes, and turned my head away. I could barely see them from the corner of my eye, but I said, "Excuse me." Janet turned to look at me with a look of exasperation as, "Are you really going to do this now, whatever it is, while I'm shopping with my sister?" She may not have been thinking that, but she looked like she wanted her space that day. I completely understood, but I also wanted them to have what they did not know they'd lost.

I said, holding out the checkbook toward Janet, "I just wanted to give you this. It was on the street." At that, I ran out the door. I could hear Janet calling "Hey!" But I was gone. I ran and ran and ran. By the time I got past the next few corners, I was breathing so hard, I couldn't breathe. Panting like a small wild animal, I realized that the Lord did not want me to run, but I could not help it. I was too broken and too scared to do anything else.

What I *did* realize is that, when we obey the voice and unction of the Holy Spirit, great things happen! Sometimes we experience the blessing right then, and sometimes later. But the point is that God never fails us! I realize that anyone could have found that checkbook, address, and bank information and wreaked havoc on that woman's life; but God would not let that be, not then. Who knows what would have happened or what would have been set in motion had I not heard the voice of the Holy Spirit and listened?

There was another time in my meditation on the Word, just before I was born again, when I do believe that I received the Lord in my room, alone. When I went to church and Pastor Lee had me pray the prayer for Salvation, I had already asked Jesus in my room to be in my life, and I had told Him that I wanted to live for Him. That was what I wrote about earlier, when the ceiling opened and I felt God's presence and began singing in "unknown tongues."

This time, I had been going to church for a while and was going to fly down to Las Vegas to spend Thanksgiving with my family. I had already booked several commercials at this time and some guest-star roles on TV.

The next day, I parked my car on the street just after the street cleaner was done. The sign indicated that we could now park on that side of the street. If you've ever lived in Los Angeles or New York or any big city, reading and comprehending street signs is crucial, because we all know that they often cross the line of honorable, to say the least.

They also seem to hire an English nerd who then flips around the syntax to make it harder to comprehend. You have rocket scientists out there, trying to figure out what the heck they really mean, and where in the heck to park!

I had already gotten several tickets and had an $800 lesson in the matter, so I parked right by my back gate, first one there and the best spot on the street. The whole block and all the buildings and house tenants were probably jealous of such a great parking space because I hit that thing five seconds after the allotted time and I could stay there safely for six more days before the parking patrol would be there again. I was in glory time! So, I was feeling cozy with my spot; my bags were in the back. I would be off to LAX, the international airport, via shuttle bus soon, and I could taste the turkey and stuffing and feel the squeeze of my brothers' strong hugs and laughter!

As I sashayed and swayed with grace toward my back gate, I heard a voice, my voice, say, "Don't park there." "What?" I'm thinking to myself that I'm just thinking too hard', right? I began to have this incredible conversation with myself (I *thought*). Now at that time I still hadn't understood that we are spirit, we have a soul, we live in a body. So when the Holy Spirit speaks to us, it is always different. Sometimes I hear His audible voice, but I'll get to that later.

When God speaks by the Holy Spirit to our spirit, our born-again spirit speaks to our soul. Our soul, which is made up of the mind, will, and emotions, then speaks to us! This is more evidence that "we are not our brain" and can cast thoughts down or keep them.

Anyway, I was having a conversation with myself (the Holy Spirit) all the way back inside the apartment. Forty-five minutes later, the shuttle was there and I was off. When I got there to Las Vegas, it was all I had hoped for; it was fantastic. While on the plane, I could still sense the impression about my car, but I just decided to "cast down evil imaginings" and put it out of my mind. But it troubled me.

Later that night, Thanksgiving Eve, I got a call from my close friend and neighbor, Donna, and she said, "Girl, have you seen the news?" I said "No." She said, "Well, L.A. is experiencing a torrential downpour, nonstop, and the street we live on used to be a riverbed." I exclaimed "*What*!?" She told me that Rossmore, where I lived, and the area close around it was just that, an old riverbed!

She then said, "Your car is floating down Rossmore Avenue and it is literally under water!" I froze...fight, flight, or freeze? I chose to freeze. I was speechless, not only about what had happened but at the power of the divine nature of God that longed to protect me from the car drama that was coming. I started to tell her the whole story, and she laughed. Well, I was upset, but I also had a kind of peace because this was not the only time that Jesus was teaching me how to hear from Him via the person of the Holy Spirit. It was the Holy Spirit He sent when He was raised from the dead, saying, "I will not leave you comfortless."

When I got home, the car looked like it had been at the bottom of a lake. It was filled with mud and leaves and twigs. It was ruined, and the whole experience gave me a very expensive lesson. My friend had towed it via AAA to the dealership. But, oh, what a friend we have in Jesus! I hadn't listened—but this taught me a deeper lesson for the future.

I have had other times just like that. For example, a similar sense of guidance occurred, but this time I listened and followed through. It was to go and see about an investment in a stock that the Holy Spirit mentioned and, believe me, I knew nothing about stocks and bonds at all. I was simply on a train along the coast in California (the Surf Liner) in order to think and hear, as I love trains and love to write. They also give you a free newspaper and punch or water in business class.

I read an article about a company that made cards for credit card companies and other organizations. The Lord said, "Buy that stock." So I decided, when I returned back home to L.A, I would do just that. A stockbroker whom I found when back in L.A., said, "No, no. That company is not good. They have debt." So I walked away confused, but still, my belly was screaming with warmth, and the impression of a message was very strong. It took me two days to even find a stockbroker because I did not know what one was or where to find them.

The time with the car was simply God and I, but this time another person was involved, another voice, the voice of the stockbroker. The stock went from $9, when I first saw it, to $36 in two weeks. The Lord was answering prayer about investments and teaching me how to trust Him and "not lean unto my own understanding." Look—when you know what to do and can see it in your heart, can see yourself doing it in a vision; it does not go away, because it is coupled with an inner witness. Do what God has said. It is often the first thought that comes to mind, but we frequently reason ourselves out of it.

> **"Only it must be in faith that he asks with no wavering (no hesitating, no doubting). For the one who wavers (hesitates, doubts) is like the billowing surge out at sea that is blown hither *and* thither and tossed by the wind. For truly, let not such a person imagine that he will receive anything [he asks for] from the Lord, [For being as he is] a man of two minds (hesitating, dubious, irresolute), [he is] unstable *and* unreliable *and* uncertain about everything [he thinks, feels, decides]."**
>
> **James 1:6-8**

Another amazing experience has occurred over the last three years. It deals with the realm of the prophetic, which is an amazing way that God speaks to us. Dreams and visions are also amazing ways that I experience God's will for me, and it is important for us to lean in and listen at all times. The prophetic is incredible, and there is too much to it to go into in this book, but I want to share a special experience. God says:

> **"He who receives *and* welcomes *and* accepts a prophet because he is a prophet shall receive a prophet's reward."**
>
> **Matthew 10:41**

There have been prophets who have spoken to me, and in this last three years, it has all been the same passionate Word from the Lord. The message has also been "words of wisdom" and "words of knowledge." One such prophet has become a dear friend, and the words she spoke and even sang were things that no one has ever known, because they are related to my deep thoughts about myself, my future, and my life. I do realize that some prophets and others with these amazing gifts and all spiritual gifts have to be very careful not to get puffed up, or too ahead of themselves. This is something I am always praying about as well, that God corrects me and does not allow me to become prideful. God's love touches us with humility, and it's good to allow ourselves to be teachable and corrected by Him. The Lord corrects those He loves, and we must receive it.

Sometimes He uses a prophet to do it, as in the case of King David and the prophet Nathan:

> **"Then Nathan said to David, You are the man! Thus says the Lord, the God of Israel: I anointed you king of Israel, and I delivered you out of the hand of Saul. And I gave you your master's house, and your master's wives into your bosom, and gave you the house of Israel and of Judah; and if that had been too little, I would have added that much again. Why have you despised the commandment of the Lord, doing evil in His sight? You have slain Uriah the Hittite with the sword and have taken his wife to be your wife. You have murdered him with the sword of the Ammonites."**
>
> **2 Samuel 12:7-9**

Wow! God loved David so much, as He loves us, that He corrected him and sent a prophet! Often we don't like being corrected, or reminded of protocol, or guided by authority.

However, in order for me to heal, I had to enjoy (or at least be humbled in) receiving *all* God's blessings, which include all of His guidance and direction. This is what Psalm 23, is all about, when it says, "Thy rod and thy staff shall comfort me." It is His gentle prodding, to lead us the right way in life. Look at what He says:

> **"And I gave you your master's house, and your master's wives into your bosom, and gave you the house of Israel and of Judah; and if that had been too little, I would have added that much again."**
>
> **2 Samuel 12:8**

He loves us so! When we are in His perfect will and in line with why we are here and what God has given us to do, He holds nothing back. I have experienced this. When we walk in His love, which is everything, everything else has to follow us, because there is nothing greater than God's love, the love of Christ.

I have had such a blessing in meeting Shanna, a prophetess from Detroit, who operates using unusual prophetic gifts. It was a challenging hour of my life. I was putting the documentary and business plan together for the drop-in center and restoration house, moving across the country for the first time, separated from my husband because of his work, and so much came against me.

I wondered if I could just run away to some distant land and do missionary work in peace. It was difficult. My marriage was strained, and I just didn't know what to do about any of it. I kept on, in prayer, fasting, and working. When nothing seemed to change as much as I needed, the Lord sent Shanna. She did not know anything about me but began to share volumes over the phone. She said the Lord kept her up and she sang a 30-minute prophecy for me into a recorder, after already speaking to me on the phone and filling me with the radiance of his love.

She sent it via email, When I heard the prophetic song, I cried and cried as if forever. Deep truths were transforming me. His love for me was evident in this, and I believed every single word! It is all coming to pass, and in such an accurate way. It was utilized by God via the Holy Spirit by the prophet to encourage, to comfort me into forward motion, and to keep traveling with force through the narrow gate, which God had set before me. I had prophecies earlier on, and these were in line with some I had heard from Dr. Beverly "Bam" Crawford years before.

I have danced and sung ever since. It does not mean there were no difficulties, but I am encouraged in great and mighty ways! It is a supernatural encouragement that only the Holy Spirit, the Spirit of God, can bring. It was so intense and the presence of the Lord so tangible as I listened, heard, and received every word. I am basking in the reward that the prophetess brought to me. I love Shanna but not because of that.

We realize that none of us will always get it right. When we submit to God's will, however, and turn away from whatever it is that we are doing wrong, He hears us. I love Shanna because she was a stranger to me, and she did not have to stop and allow the Lord, my Lord, to use her, but she did—and with a grace and love that I will always cherish and admire. She is unique, with a “heart in her eye” to prove it.

There are many ways in which God speaks to us, and we need to spend time with Him to be able to hear. The Lord longs to spend time with us, with you, and this is why I stressed this more than once! Won't you ask Him and see? For anything else to try and compete with His love, it would have to be greater. It’s not, so that's when we go from “glory to glory” and His blessings overtake us.

It is so very important to listen, hear, and follow through with what God is leading us to do by His Spirit. A relationship with the Holy Spirit is key to this, as well as learning to sharpen our ears to Him. Especially when we have trust issues and are building our lives, we need to know that we can trust God. We can trust what He says about who we are even if we don't believe it ourselves, because if He said it, it's true. He will show us that it is so if we only trust Him and “lean not unto our own understanding but acknowledge Him, He will direct our paths” (Proverbs 3:5-6 KJV).

As He directs our paths in life, He has to direct the pathways of our minds and hearts, because the issues of life, according to Scripture, come from such. When our mind and heart "paths," our thinking, our chemical balance of neurotransmitters and hormones, are transformed by God, and healthy new paths are formed, we can praise Him and share it along the way. Then the path we take in life, down whatever pathways He leads and sends us through, will be sound and exceptional! They will be full of promise, purpose, and fulfilled destiny. Moreover, it will be about His kingdom, and *many*, because of your work in God, will learn of His saving Grace. That, my Beloved, is what it is all about.

On this side of heaven we should enjoy life, because it is a gift, but what is the fun if we don't share it?

Praise Corner

> **Praise you, Lord, for your amazing brilliance and the way in which you are showing us the way. Thank you for not giving up on us, Father, and loving us *more* than we even understand sometimes, for words cannot describe it! Praise your Holy Name forever!**

Whenever the enemy comes in like a flood, whether in the spirit, against your mind, or in the natural world, Mark 13:11 states:

> **"Now when they take you [to court] and put you under arrest, do not be anxious beforehand about what you are to say *nor* [*even*] *meditate about it*; but say whatever is given you in that hour *and* at the moment, for it is not you who will be speaking, but the Holy Spirit."**

God will tell us what to say, what to pray, and how to

handle any difficult situation that arises. On the other side of a "test" is a "testimony," a monologue of how great your God is. He sometimes has to bring us to a place where there is no one there but Him (or almost), so you know that He is for you and will defend you.

This is what we must know in order to be whole and to walk in and accomplish the incredible dreams and desires that He has placed in us with fullness of joy and success! Take heed and listen to the Holy Spirit and sharpen your ears, natural and spiritual, for:

> **"So then faith comes by hearing, and hearing by the Word of God."**
>
> **Romans 10:17 (KJV)**

> **"And the Word (Christ) became flesh (human, incarnate) and tabernacle (fixed His tent of flesh, lived awhile) among us; and we [actually] saw His glory (His honor, His majesty), such glory as an only begotten son receives from his father, full of grace (favor, loving-kindness) and truth."**
>
> **John 1:14**

He is ever present and right there to help you, heal you, and give you victory in life. I am a living witness of His restorative power. I am not saying that there is no pain or sorrow in my life; however, I am saying that He sees you and me through it all, and His joy has become my strength. You know how powerful the Holy Spirit is, and what He can accomplish in you, for you, and around you. Look at what He did with Mary:

> **"Then the angel said to her, The Holy Spirit will come upon you, and the power of the Most High will overshadow you [like a shining cloud]; and so**

the holy (pure, sinless) Thing (Offspring) which shall be born *of you* will be called the Son of God.'"

Luke 1:35

I have heard His voice audibly, and it shook me. I have heard angelic singing early in the morning when no one was there but my God. He has said to me, "Go," on a day when church was the last place I wanted to go, but when I went, it was the first place I needed to be.

It was as if the pastor had read all my mail! I'm writing songs now for healing hearts; I hear them in the early morning and sometimes in my dreams. My hope is to do as the Spirit wills, what He has called me to do, and that is to cast out darkness! Raise the dead of all kinds of death in various forms in life! Heal infirmities! I believe that when He asks me to do it, wherever and whenever, He will go before me and I will be there. This is my hope, to see God's people whole and free! To see those who don't believe in God also whole and free, for He said:

"Believe Me that I am in the Father and the Father in Me; or else believe Me for the sake of the [very] works themselves. [If you cannot trust Me, at least let these works that I do in My Father's name convince you]."

John 14:11

And I know and believe that He does them, His works, through us His children, and as we yield our lives and let go of all else, miracles happen. All we have to do is notice and appreciate them while giving God all of the glory.

> the holy (pure, sinless) Thing (Offspring) which shall be born of you will be called the Son of God."
>
> Luke 1:35

I have heard His voice audibly, and it spoke to me. I have heard angelic singing early in the morning when no one was there but my God. He has said to me, [illegible] which church was the best place to attend [illegible] was the first place I [illegible]

[illegible]

[illegible] through us His children [illegible] paradise [illegible] all we [illegible]

12

The Need for Fathers: Lifting Up and Respecting Men of Honor

"And the Lord God took the man and put him in the Garden of Eden to tend and guard and keep it."

Genesis 2:15

I had always longed as a little girl for a father who would be there for me. As with many American children and others in the world, divorce, fighting, anger, remarriage, domestic violence, and fathers who find themselves overworked, got in the way of my natural father and stepfathers, preventing them from being there for me. I did not grow up being raised by my dad. I wonder what it would be like to have a father who was and is always there. I am sure that many children and adults wonder this very thing.

According to various studies, the absence of a loving father can be extremely harmful in profound ways to the life of a child and, later, an adult. It is all right to cry about it and grow from there, because it is a loss, and it is not the way God intended it to be. And yet He is the excellent Father and has made a way for all of us to be lacking in nothing, as we yield to Him. I want to finish this chapter with something written by my spiritual father, but first, look at some of these statistics with me. They speak volumes on the importance of a father's presence in their childrens' entire lives.

The following information comes from *The Importance of Fathers: Statistical compilation by the South Carolina Fathers Initiative* by Keith Pounds, MBA:

Child custody & visitation:

- **As many as 50% of custodial mothers admit to interfering with father visitation in order to "punish" the father (Arditti, 1992; Braver, 2011; Miller & Knox, 2001).** [
- **Among children living in single-mother homes, 35% never see their fathers and 24% see their father only once per month (Pruett et al., 2000).**
- **Conventional parenting plans allow children to live with their fathers only about 15% of the time (Nielson, 2011; Sonenstein et al., 2002).**
- **70% of fathers feel like they have too little time with their children and the vast majority of children want more time with their fathers (Ahrons, 2004; Fabricus, 2003; Finely & Schwartz, 2007; Kock & Lowery, 1984; Hallman & Deinhart, 2007).**
- **23% of children in the U.S. live with their mother only, 5% live with their father only, and 3% live with neither parent (Note: As many children live with no parent as live with their father only) (Fields, 2003).**

- Those children who enjoy the benefit of "Shared Parenting" rate equally or better in psychological, academic, behavioral, and social well-being compared to those in traditional post-divorce custody (Aquilino, 2010; Breivik & Olweus, 2006; Scott et al., 2007; Melli & Brown, 2008).

Crime and Behavior:

- A young male's likelihood of engaging in criminal activity 'triples' if he is reared in a neighborhood with a high concentration of single-parent families (Baskerville, 2002; Baskerville, 2004).

Children from fatherless homes constitute:

- 80% of rapists motivated by "displaced anger" (Knight & Prentky, 1987).
- 63% of youth suicides (Brent et al., 1995).
- 72% adolescent murders (Cornell et al., 1987; Davidson, 1990; McNeely, 1988).
- 70-85% of youths in state prisons (Cornell et al., 1987; Knight & Prentky, 1987; Wells & Rankin, 1991).
- 80% of adolescent patients (Block, 1988) suffer disproportionately from, and are much more likely to be treated for, a variety of psychological and behavioral disorders as compared to those from intact families (Aquilino, 2010; Breivik & Olweus, 2006; Brent, 1995; Hanson et al., 1996; Lee, 2002; McNelly, 1998; Melli & Brown, 2008; Phares & Lum, 1997; Prazen et al., 2011; Scott et al., 2007; Spruijt & Duindam, 2009).

- They also: **Are much more likely to exhibit violent, aggressive, and criminal behavior (Vaden-Kierman, et al., 1995).**
- **Display worse behavior when incarcerated (Marshall et al., 2001).**
- **Have higher rates of mental illness, violence, and alcohol and drug use (Berman 1995 Duncan et al., 1994) and engage in greater and even earlier sexual activity (Metzler et al., 1994).**

<u>Children from two-parent homes are:</u>

- **Twice as likely to graduate from high school, even when taking into account race, socioeconomic status, and other factors (Luster & Mcadoo, 1994)**
- **20 times as likely to attend college (Wallerstein and Tanke, 1986).**

<u>Domestic violence & child abuse:</u>

- **Children living in homes where the biological father is not present are at much greater risk to suffer from child abuse (Halpern-Meeking & Tach, 2008).**[1]

We get a clear picture as we read the following:

"God said, Let Us [Father, Son, and Holy Spirit] make mankind in Our image, after Our likeness, and let them have complete authority over the fish of the sea, the birds of the air, the [tame] beasts, and over all of the earth, and over everything that creeps upon the earth

Genesis 1:26

Notice that mankind has *authority* over all the earth, so what happens in it is a result of the *action of man*.

The Bible teaches us that Adam named all of the animals on Earth, which shows the supernatural intelligence and insight to the things and purposes of the earth and of God. There is debate whether man and woman were male and female at creation. However, the answer is not found in the way dysfunctional minds think when they debate it in the first place. Scripture is clear when it states:

> **"He created them male and female and blessed them and named them [both] Adam [Man] at the time they were created."**
>
> **Genesis 5:2**

All this means is that mankind is important to God. That male and female are a part of one another, which is why good marriages and loving fathers are important.

Healthy women and men understand how important they are in the raising of children, but many men don't always seem to have the same understanding that they are just as important.

Men have their own unique position; that in no way makes women less important, because women have always had to be there for their children. Woman was also with Man before the rib was removed, because God had a plan. God the Father took the rib from Adam's side and Adam called her Woman.

> **"And the Lord God caused a deep sleep to fall upon Adam; and while he slept, He took one of his ribs *or* a part of his side and closed up the [place with] flesh. And the rib *or* part of his side which the Lord God had taken from the man He built up *and***

> **made into a woman, and He brought her to the man. Then Adam said, This [creature] is now bone of my bones and flesh of my flesh; she shall be called Woman, because she was taken out of a man."**
>
> **Genesis 2:21-23**

Powerful! Mankind is highly intelligent, which is why we are so important to one another. It is also why, when we cause pain, especially to those we love, it creates great trauma in the makeup of who we were created to be.

Not only did Adam name all living things, even before woman was taken supernaturally from one of his ribs, but Adam gave women the very name *woman*! He also gave her the name Eve, or "life spring," as one translation defines it.

> **"And Adam called his wife's name Eve; because she was the mother of all living."**
>
> **Genesis 3:20 (KJV)**

She is and was, "life spring." There is such an order to things. The Word of God says:

> **"So those who [now] are last will be first [then], and those who [now] are first will be last [then]. For many are called, but few chosen."**
>
> **Matthew 20:16**

Respect and honor to men is also due because of their love and care toward us. The Bible says that there is no greater love than to

> **"lay down (give up) his own life for his friends.!"**
>
> **John 15:13**

Oh what a friend we have in Jesus!

Scripture is clear that man is to,

> **"Love his wife, like Christ loves the church and gave his life for her."**
>
> **Ephesians 5:25**

This is powerful, and I perceive that when women experience this type of love, they will love and respect and honor men all the more.

I believe that men are a powerful answer to the issue of modern day slavery and human trafficking, for they are also the biggest perpetrators of these terrible crimes against women, and children. I believe it is men of honor who must rise up and pull lost men—fathers, sons, brothers—from the hell of their unchecked perversions such as using little girls for sex and buying and selling the bodies of girls and women. Men must rise up and take a vertical position of truth, in love, and lead alongside the women who desperately need to know that they are there.

> **"So God created man in his own image, in the image of God he created him; male and female He created them."**
>
> **Genesis: 1:27**

Now, Beloved, the next few words may seem difficult for some of you, but I am only giving you an idea of what is going on. What happens when things go awry?

> **"And they have cast lots for my people; and have given a boy for an harlot, and sold a girl for wine, that they might drink."**
>
> **Joel 3:3 (KJV)**

This is what is happening now in many places. Young girls, boys, and of course women are being sold to be raped and soul-assassinated. There are "baby farms" in parts of the world. Young women are taken, kidnapped, and enslaved. They are raped and raped and impregnated to bear the children of this crime, to be sold into this vortex of unimaginable evil: selling a baby to be raped.

This is a fact. Of course, now that we know as much as we do about human trafficking/modern day slavery, it is no surprise what traffickers/pedophiles do in order to make the billions of dollars they do, and to fulfill demonic desires of their perverted customers.

> **"This know also, that in the last days perilous times shall come. For men shall be lovers of their own selves, covetous, boasters, proud, blasphemers, disobedient to parents, unthankful, unholy, Without natural affection, truce breakers, false accusers, incontinent, fierce, despisers of those that are good, traitors, heady, high minded, lovers of pleasures more than lovers of God; Having a form of godliness, but denying the power thereof: from such turn away."**
>
> **2 Timothy 3 (KJV)**

This Scripture is not gender-specific, but it does describe the importance of the love of a family and protecting our loved ones and our children. It states with severity that serving God is all that matters, because all good things are born of and come from Him and Him alone. We are to be mindful of who we are and who we are to be.

His joy is our strength. Living a life full of His joy is very important. He is caring for us; and because He is, He will guide us to do what is right and good in Him so all forms of slavery end. I realize some say "I'm not going to see it," but faith is not about what others think, nor about what I see. It's about fighting for something we believe in. This Evil happening to our children, and the violence and abuse happening to women (at the hands of men) must end, and we must do it together! The children who do not get help grow up to be adults who are lost and hurt, likely for a lifetime. Some survive, emotionally; some don't. Many become criminals, perpetuating the vicious cycle. It's time to share the love of God. It's time for fathers to turn their hearts back and for mothers, even those upset over divorce, with all the complex emotions and issues involved, to allow the father into his children's lives, when he is willing, loving, and true.

> "**And he will [himself] go before Him in the spirit and power of Elijah, to turn back the hearts of the fathers to the children...".**
>
> **Luke 1:17**

The following is written for this book by my spiritual father Dr. Carroll A. Baltimore, Sr. He has been in ministry for more than 45 years. I asked him to share his heart as it relates to men and fathers, because he is one of God's best.

"In Dr. Martin Luther King, Jr.'s, book, *The Measure of a Man*, he defines man as 'God's marvelous creation. Through his mind he can leap oceans, break through walls, and transcend the categories of time and space.'

"When I recall this statement by Dr. King, I think of Brook. Her resiliency and ability to leap over the oceans of despair, break through the walls that were constantly caving in around her, transcend her mind past time and space to gain her freedom, and to transition into a type of Moses, leading young girls and women and even men trapped in human trafficking and sexual abuse to freedom, exemplifies Dr. King's statement. This is something that many have tried to accomplish, but against all odds, Brook is a shining example of this great achievement.

"The definition of man has been debated since the fall of man. God created man in his own image, with his own hands, and with his own breath. He had a specific goal in mind for man and the world that he created. Man was to be the caretaker of the earth, beasts of the field, fowl of the air, and creatures in the sea. He also created man to care for and provide the necessities of life for the woman and all forms of life. He also created man to care for and provide the necessities of sustenance for the woman and their descendants. There was to be harmony and mutual care for the world, and the world would produce all the food and necessities for man and his family to live. But something went wrong…they believed the lie, rather than believe in God. Thus, the death of all humankind began.

"Since that time, man has been all out of sorts as to his true role and responsibilities. Throughout history, and our own lives, we have many examples of what not to do as a man and how to be a great man. But again, what is the definition of a man, his role and responsibility? You can ask 100 people, and get 100 different definitions. The response will be derived from the context of their cultural surroundings, home environment, and personal experiences. Personally, I was raised with many Godly examples of men.

"From a Godly perspective, we find additional instructions relating to the responsibilities of man, in addition to the things we have previously mentioned. Man is also to be the priest in the home, to love, provide for, and protect his wife and family.

"Being a priest in the home not only refers to the godly lessons and instructions given in the home, but also the character and lifestyle exemplified in his job, in the Church, and the community.

"As a child, I was influenced by strong, yet humble men of responsibility. As children, we were never provoked, bullied, or punished unjustifiably. We were never abused physically, verbally, or sexually. We were taught that life is sacred, and that we are to respect and protect the life of our sisters and brothers.

"We were taught to be peaceful in nature, but not timid or afraid. We were taught that dialogue, rather than fighting, was always the first approach to problem-solving. We worked as children, learning to take ownership of our actions, responsibility in sharing the workload and chores, and other simple tasks in the community. I was taught the biblical difference between right and wrong and how to conduct myself in daily life according to Scripture. I constantly witnessed a lifestyle of righteousness through integrity, honesty, respect for leadership, and reverence for God. The prayer and Bible study in my home, along with the reinforcement that God will bring you out of each challenge in life that you face, has benefited me in life and ministry.

"There were always life's lessons in everything that we did. All of the teaching and influence from godly males in my family has helped to shape me into the man that I am today. I am so thankful for my humble beginnings as a child and adolescent years, because it helped me to truly understand that God created man to worship Him.

"Worshipping God does not just take place in our houses of worship, but is to be a lifestyle of worship.

"We worship God in our tempered speech, our words of instruction and rebuke that are solely motivated by love for God and for all people.

"We worship God with our ability to make biblically sound decisions, along with just and fair judgments that are based on the truth and not hearsay or gossip.

"We worship God by counting/calculating the cost and long-term effects of our decisions on our family and others.

"Man worships God with his life and all that he has.

"Not all individuals have been blessed to have shining examples of real men with a lifestyle of worship. That is why our world is so misguided regarding the real definition, role, and responsibilities of a man. Many of today's men have grown up without good father figures or fathers at all. Because of the incredible void this presents, we are left with boys and young men getting their examples from the street gangs or other unsuitable sources. We all have the deep desire to be loved and to belong to a family unit. Unfortunately, as these young men try to develop other relationships, they fail miserably. The ability to cope with responsibility and have good interpersonal and communication skills with others is lacking. They lack the ability to show respect for mankind in general. Unfortunately, this is why Brook has to tell her story.

"In the foothills of Virginia, there would almost always be a rainbow after a good rain shower. We were told as children that a pot of gold was at the end of the rainbow. Our family was poor, and with great expectation we waited to see the rainbow. We would run through the field and do our best to reach the end of the rainbow to the pot of gold. Getting that pot of gold would mean no more poverty and we could move off of the mountain into the city. My parents would no longer have to work from sunup to sundown. As children, our parents could not afford to buy us clothes that actually fit and that were not two sizes too large. What an exciting thought! It would mean freedom from so many unfortunate circumstances in life that we had to bear. But as we ran, we could never reach the end of that rainbow…it seemed to elude us.

So, we would give up and go back home to the same existence as before.

"However, I can say that Brook believed that she would find a pot of gold at the end of her rainbow. She never stopped trying. She did what it took to be free from her unfortunate circumstances. She found her pot of gold and is doing all that she can to make life better for other girls, boys, women, and men also. She continues to rescue them from their tragedies, and encourages them to reach their own pot of gold to freedom in their soul, mind, and body. She teaches how to use tragedies as a launching pad to greatness.

"I leave with you the passage of Scripture that has become my anchor and assurance for the many obstacles and endeavors that I face daily and will face in the future, Ephesians 3:20:

"'Now to Him Who, by the [action of His] power that is at work within us, is able to [carry out His purpose and] do superabundantly, far over *and* above all that we [dare] ask or think [infinitely beyond our highest prayers, desires, thoughts, hopes, or dreams].'"

Dr. Carroll A. Baltimore, Sr.

13

OUR LANGUAGE IS OUR LIFE

As well as healing and changing our lives after abuse and challenges, we must also change our very language about these related issues, if we are truly to thrive. There are only a few things about this issue that I will share now, as a more comprehensive treatment will be in a book to follow.

I have fought in many areas to be clear about where I'm going and where God says I am, rather than focus on what I feel or often see in my life. I may see it with my eyes, but I can't let this enter my heart for long, without coming to my senses and *counteracting* that doubting, negative, powerless thought or statement with something hopeful. I will not declare it or give it power if it does not line up with God's Word and what the Holy Spirit has shared with me.

We often say so many unproductive, complaining, and/or fearful and hopeless things; and then we say to a friend, in response to a *comeback statement*, "Well, I know, but I didn't mean it that way," or "I know, but I had to explain it so that you would understand," or "I know, but it's how I feel." However, there are more positive ways to express a challenging situation that speak the truth and also the hope of coming out of it with victory!

For example, if someone asked how I was feeling and I knew what the doctor had said and I knew what God had said, I could say, "The doctor said I have a bad knee," and it does hurt, but I know that sickness cannot dwell in the "temple of the Holy Spirit" and stay there long. I know this, because it is written:

> **"And thus He fulfilled what was spoken by the prophet Isaiah, He Himself took [in order to carry away] our weaknesses *and* infirmities and bore away our diseases."**
>
> **Matthew 8:17**

So, I may do whatever my doctor says, do physical therapy, take care of myself, and *also* pray, lay hands on the knee, and speak the Word of God, but I will not speak out loud a declaration of illness. While I am doing the practical things prescribed by my doctor or physical therapist, I am also praying, and I believe in the healing power of God as well. I know that, if not today, then tomorrow, I will experience breakthrough and healing in that knee. And even if I did not, I would still keep believing God! I have done this and been like this for a long while, and I will remain so. Sometimes healing is instant; sometimes it's not, but it is as the Spirit wills, and I trust the Holy Spirit. I know that God is for me, and if God is for me, who or what can be against me?

Whether in the body or in society, illness is often brought on by our words, our thinking, our language. Even in medicine and psychology, it is taught that a very large percentage of illnesses are psychosomatic. Whether true or not, I'd rather speak in a positive way of life as much as possible, rather than from a negative and defeatist mindset.

The words *prostitute* or *prostitution*, for instance, are used in reference to what some call an *industry*; the issue of human trafficking is often placed within the now popularly coined terminology of "the sex-industry."

But the term *sex-industry* is a gross misnomer. Consider this: Merriam-Webster's Online Dictionary defines *industry* as "systematic labor especially for some useful purpose or the creation of something of value," and "a department or branch of a craft, art, business, or manufacture.

So is child rape and violent trauma creating something of value for society? Is drugging, beating, violating, selling, and buying the bodies of girls and women a craft, an art? Are these for some wholesome, useful purpose, as the dictionary suggests? Is the trafficking, this degradation and destruction of bodies and minds—which creates billions of dollars in profits for the pimps, the madams, the traffickers—an "INDUSTRY"?

When we use sanitizing terminology and language like this, we commercialize—and worse, we normalize—unspeakably perverted acts, systematic barbaric violence, and degradation and humiliation of girls, boys, women, and men, all of whom who are caught, dehumanized in the poisonous spider web of human trafficking.

We create problems, especially for young, underdeveloped minds that are evolving into the personalities of their more mature lives. The human brain cannot automatically decipher words which are popularly used for something society considers good—or at least normal, ordinary, a state of affairs that has always existed. On the contrary—these abuses are, and have always been, nothing more than vicious crimes.

In addition, the fact that prostitution is accepted by the unfortunate and foolish doesn't mean we must use this word to describe it. I much prefer "a prostituted person." Albeit, in Scripture, it speaks of the "great whore or prostitute" who is a spirit neither male nor female. (Revelations 17:5). When we normalize language, we create confusion. How can using a child's body for sex, or sex slavery, be "sex" at all, when the root word for sex *Koinonia* is *intimacy*? It's rape slavery and nothing more. Out of obstinate denial of the horrific truth, or out of willful ignorance of its destructiveness, people have termed it so, but it is not what God intended. God created sex, intimacy, for a purpose, and rape and the impurity of even sexual sport is not that purpose.

How can the auto industry use the same word as something that murders, rapes, and violates every human right known to man? How can some call selling bodies "sex work," or those who do it "sex workers" when these acts are not "work"?

Do we call those who rob banks *workers*?

What about pedophiles who rape? Is what they do *work*? What about kidnappers—do they *work*? Money does change hands, after all, but is it *work*?

Just because some women over 18 or 21 have made an unhealthy decision to sell their bodies doesn't mean this choice at some point was not "forced prostitution."

We should not use language to normalize the fact that prostitution legal or otherwise degrades and destroys victims of all ages, and that those who are enmeshed on either side are broken and lost. And who does it really benefit?

There are so many things that need to change about how we label what is sheer, numbing agony for so many thousands; and we need to change how we label one another.

I never felt as bad at any time in all that happened to me as when I experienced what call *revictimization.*

I remember going to a doctor who had heard of my film documentary about freedom and human trafficking, and he said, "You were trafficked? Oh, I mean, you were a prostitute?"

This careless statement hit all of the painful, discordant notes in my heart that I had almost forgotten. I wanted to walk out of the office, I felt so hurt. But I didn't. I just thought, "We have work to do."

I might say that every victim of sex slavery is often a domestic slave as well, because we have to perform household chores too.

I was never a prostitute, let me be clear. I was a victim of *child rape slavery* and soul assassination, a crude and evil form of human trafficking/modern day slavery. But to be thought of only as an eventual survivor would mean that I was stuck there, identified only as such. I wanted to soar beyond that state. So, in my evolution, I became a *thriver,* and now I am simply a "champion." I am a champion as anyone is who struggles through a grueling battle to victory. And I could only have achieved this with God's love and guidance.

I say about myself what King David said about himself:

> **"I will praise thee; for I am fearfully and wonderfully made: marvelous are thy works; and that my soul knoweth right well."**
>
> **Psalms 139:14 (KJV)**

**GOD HAS PREPARED A WAY FOR US
NO MATTER WHAT HAS HAPPENED**

14

RECONCILIATION

"It was God [personally present] in Christ, reconciling *and* restoring the world to favor with Himself, not counting up *and* holding against [men] their trespasses [but canceling them], and committing to us the message of reconciliation (of the restoration to favor)."

2 Corinthians 5:19

Only God-led leadership, rooted in the wisdom of experience and being in accord in love, can heal this disorder in our society. Only the understanding that God is a forgiving God who has reconciled us to Himself, can make us be clean as snow, sanctified and cleansed by the precious blood of the Lamb. And we must pay this love forward, along the way; we must reach out, each in our own way, to do what we can to hearten, comfort, and help others in distress.

"You may not always have a comfortable life and you will not always be able to solve all of the world's problems at once but don't ever underestimate the importance you can have because history

has shown us that courage can be contagious and hope can take on a life of its own."

Michelle Obama,
Lawyer, Health Advocate,
1st lady of USA, wife of 44th pres.

God has created life so that we can live together, work, build, and resolve issues like racism, and a loss of social tolerance and mutual respect in community. Not everyone is a believer in God, but these issues need a moral compass. How do we do that together, so that we as a country can work together in a way that makes sense? It doesn't matter whether we are Democrat or Republican, we simply need to be human and fellow citizens..

There is no such thing as the "Christian Right"; all believers are woven in and throughout society and political opinion. Sometimes I think, "WWJD?": *What would Jesus do?* If we wear the bracelet, I guess we at least have to try and do what He did. I clearly remember what He said to the tormentors who surrounded the cross: "Father, forgive them, for they know not what they do" (Luke 23:34. KJV).

We have got to find some way to come together, to forgive, and to *work together* on these all of these issues as well as rape and sex-slavery, as well as similar forms of sexual and physical violence perpetrated also on young men in prison, kids in foster care, and incarcerated girls and women. We must grapple with the evils of incest, molestation, domestic violence, and rape done by fathers and other family members to their children and wives as well. After all, that is the message of Christ!

Whether Black or White or any ethnic group or religious creed, it really doesn't matter. The Lord does not love just one of His children, but all of them. I realize that we are living in challenging times, but that's what makes faith so powerful! With God, all things are possible. Champions should be supported as healthy, powerful advocates for positive change in our troubled world, have the greatest opportunity and scope to express to others how they have gotten through. What one non-survivor lacks in theory, we are able to communicate, from our neck-down experience—and the neck-up as well, for that matter.

Anyone can be taught a neck-up theory, but the neck-down exposure and experience cannot be taught. Thus, we must be at the leaders' table, especially with men and women who work with us.

Moreover, those who have not had a neck-down experience call certain adolescent victims "hard to deal with." But champions are more thoughtful, recalling where we were, and we call them "broken" and "unaware."

Many have been asleep regarding modern-day slavery for so long and the Bible says:

> **"For there is nothing hidden that shall not be disclosed, nor anything secret that shall not be known and come out into the open."**
>
> **Luke 8:17**

But how?

> **"It is the glory of God to conceal a thing, but the glory [honor] of kings is to search out a thing."**
>
> **Proverbs 25:2**

We have to seek it out with all of our heart, through the deep recesses of our minds; that is when transformation takes place, which is then our honor to share.

Yes, we need "safe harbor laws in every state. A safe harbor law is " a provision of a statute or a regulation that specifies that certain conduct will be deemed not to violate a given rule."[2] This means that teenaged girls or boys no longer will be locked up for any form of prostitution. Can I get an Amen on that!? And it means that women who were arrested for prostitution or loitering, but who were either trafficked or violated as minors, will not be locked up but, rather, able to enter into a healthy restoration program. It could be one like ours; More Too Life, 941-227-1012, **www.moretoolife.org**, or a program like the effective ones started by dear friends of mine and listed on my website. You will note that I closely partner with a few.

With all of the rescues and stings in the USA, these children and women need a place to go and heal—a place run by people who truly understand what they've been through. These are often champion-run programs. There are other programs, but unless a person has become a healthy survivor, that individual is not assisting former victims of human trafficking. At More Too Life, we focus on all forms of human trafficking and its root causes; as you will discover, they all collide.

In writing this book, I was researching what others were saying about root causes of these issues. And in a dream or vision I had, the evil one, darkness himself, laughed at the fact that he is The Trafficker. He has been trafficking souls through the "broad gate of destruction" for a very long time. As I quoted earlier:

> **"Narrow is the gate that leads to life and there be few who will find it."**
>
> **Matthew 7:13-14**

I realized in the vision that the hidden truths of human trafficking and abuse reveal the hidden sins of society. Not just of the tricks, pimps, traffickers, and pedophiles but of those of us in society who have watched it go on day after day.

> **"An adulterous generation requires a sign but they cannot discern the signs of the times."**
>
> **Matthew 16:4**

Often, we have wanted a sign, a message of how to make money, of where to live, what car to buy, what house to move to—or even of where to build a new church.

But God says:

> **"…seek ye first the kingdom of God and all these things will be added unto thee."**
>
> **Matthew 6:33**

It is important to succeed with what we are given to do while we are here on earth, yes, and to have fun in life doing it. It is also important, however, to do as it says in Mark 12:31 and love our neighbors as ourselves.

When we love like Abba, Daddy, like our heavenly Father loves, on even a small level, He reveals some things, and as He reveals, we fight injustice, we are impelled to

> **"[Strive to] save others, snatching [them] out of [the] fire."**
>
> **Jude 1:23**

Human trafficking/modern day slavery. are a hidden revelation of what time it really is in todays world, and while we need to be rid of slavery, and we have to treat the symptoms, we also have to seek out their root issues and heal our own souls at the same time.

> **"Whenever our hearts in [tormenting] self-accusation make us feel guilty *and* condemn us. [For we are in God's hands.] For He is above *and* greater than our consciences (our hearts), and He knows (perceives and understands) everything [nothing is hidden from Him]. And, beloved, if our consciences (our hearts) do not accuse us [if**

they do not make us feel guilty and condemn us], we have confidence (complete assurance and boldness) before God."

1 John 3:20-21

His love will lead us to the clearing field. There are women, girls, men, and boys who have never told they were raped. The fact that we don't tell is part of the problem. If we can be rid of the shame and guilt of what we think was our fault and never was, we no longer give place to darkness. Then we will, as Scripture says,

"Leave no [such] room *or* foothold for the devil [give no opportunity to him]."

Ephesians 4:27

The ills of rape will not go away if we bury it deep in our minds and hearts. The thoughts we engage affect us, even into our genes and cells. Wrong thoughts and actions are passed on in ways that cause illness to us, our bodies, our souls, and, ultimately, to our society.

We, as champions who have survived and evolved past all forms of human trafficking, and all who have been abused, cannot compare our lives or our experiences with those of others.

We shouldn't even try. We have so much to live for! There is no comparison to anyone, as all of us are so uniquely different and beautifully created.

You were born for greatness and to be an answer to a problem for someone, somewhere; and regardless of the past, if you stay on track, you will get there. It's coming!

The few Scriptures below remind me of the many champions who have escaped all forms of human trafficking.

And I add those of you who have been pimped by darkness for far too long—even you can be born anew. You can walk away from pornography, domestic violence, drug addition, stealing, lying, cheating, selfishness, anger, despair, vain desires—all that misery—to seek the love of God!

You can begin to live the life you were born to, because that is what God intends for us.

That is what freedom is and why Jesus the Christ defied death for you. He showed us that we could transform our minds, our hearts, our lives. We can die to the old ways of the flesh and old thinking and old life, to be born and live anew, again and again in Him. We can change in His love.

> **"Except the Lord of hosts had left us a very small remnant [of survivors], we should have been like Sodom, and we should have been like Gomorrah."**
>
> **Isaiah 1:9**

> **"And whoever shall call on the name of the Lord shall be delivered *and* saved, for in Mount Zion and in Jerusalem there shall be those who escape, as the Lord has said, and among the remnant [of survivors] shall be those whom the Lord calls."**
>
> **Joel 2:32**

> **"And you hath he quickened, who were dead in trespasses and sins; Wherein in time past ye walked according to the course of this world, according to the prince of the power of the air, the spirit that now worketh in the children of disobedience: Among whom also we all had our conversation in times past in the lusts of our flesh, fulfilling the desires of the flesh and of the mind; and were by nature the children of wrath, even as others. But**

> **God, who is rich in mercy, for his great love wherewith he loved us."**
>
> **Ephesians 2:1-4 (KJV)**

He can change our very nature! A child with an underdeveloped heart and mind is still a gentle flower, an innocent who must be protected. Nevertheless, aren't we all God's children? We can no longer have "a form of godliness, but having denied the power therefore" (2 Timothy 3:5). His power can do this with us; we can do this in Him. So, I had to die after all. I had to die to what I thought was desirable, and die to all the pain and rapes that I had experienced. I had to die to all of the lost years along the way. I had to die to fleshly dreams and desires that I thought would cure my ills. I had to die to self so that I could be reborn again and again and again, in Him. How did I die when I already felt dead? In a word, I had to believe. I had to discover the good work that God placed in me, work and a destiny that is discovered only by surrendering to His will. I had to trust that He could bring it to pass.

> **"And I am convinced *and* sure of this very thing, that He Who began a good work in you will continue until the day of Jesus Christ [right up to the time of His return], developing [that good work] *and* perfecting *and* bringing it to full completion in you."**
>
> **Philippians 1:6**

Who knew that my life would be a hidden treasure my Lord was waiting to show me! In Him, my life would be my treasure found on the other side of the rainbow. The rainbow in the sky throughout my life would be a glimpse into His presence.

"And he that sat was to look upon like a jasper and a sardine stone: and there was a rainbow round about the throne, in sight like unto an emerald."

Revelation 4:3 (KJV)

15

ABOUT THE AUTHOR

LOOK AT GOD IN ME NOW
LIVING ABOVE THE RAINBOW!

Dr. Brook Parker-Bello is an ordained minister, filmmaker, actress, author, CEO/Executive Director of a visionary NGO, More Too Life, a Mentoring and Identity Discovery Center for victims of all forms of Human Trafficking, also rape, incest, and prostitution. We include Demand Prevention, Community Prevention and Awareness, Outreach, and the Mentoring of youth 10 and up.

Dr. Bello is a champion, an author, motivational speaker, and human rights activist. She is a appointed member of the research advisory council for Hunt Alternative's Demand Abolition, and its important work, along with noted and key leaders. She recently received her Doctor of Letters degree from Richmond Virginia Seminary and Bishop, Chancellor, and Pastor Dr. Leonard N. Smith.

She has spoken at the White House Plenary Session, "White House Summit to Eradicate Modern Day Slavery."

Dr. Bello has spoken and preached sermons in many settings, including women's seminars. She teaches through her story and the Scriptures.

She enjoys taking the message of God into and outside the walls of the church by sharing her unique process of healing with others. She has spoken alongside governors, senators, legislators, leaders, church leaders, and others, including Congresswoman Gwen Moore and political analyst Donna Brazile. Dr. Bello has spoken to audiences composed of leading CEO's, heads of nations and churches, and families and friends. Her vision and story of survival, and her life pursuit to see others free, has been featured in a number of magazines including *Essence* and *Ebony*. ABC-TV, *700 Club*, and dozens of other newspapers and e-zines have also featured her story and message.

Dr. Brook Bello is a 2014 recipient of the Skinner Institute Scholarship for the Masters Series for Distinguished Leaders.

She is the 2013 recipient of the Presidents Award from the Progressive National Baptist Convention, the home of Dr. Martin Luther King, Jr.

Assistant Attorney General Leyser Hayes, an AKA Sorority, new trafficking initiative M.I.N.D.S (Merciful Intervention Now Demands Safety) after being inspired by watching Dr. Bello speak.

Dr. Bello's passion is to see women and children free from the injustice of human trafficking and many other forms of abuse. She emphasizes prevention, awareness, and outreach work, and also is formulating plans to open a drop-in center.

Her groundbreaking film *Survivor* is a true-life documentary about her personal story of healing from the sex trade, sex slavery, and abuse. It premiered at the 65th Annual Festival de Cannes in a private screening at Cinema du Monde, where Dr. Bello spoke to an international audience.

Dr. Bello was ordained by her pastor, author, Dr. Beverly "Bam" Crawford of Bible Enrichment Fellowship Church, in Los Angeles California.

She has worked on more than ten TV shows in more than 68 episodes. Dr. Bello had a starring role in *Stargate SG-1*, playing Dreay Auc, wife of Teal C.

Dr. Bello has worked with many notable actors and directors, including Angela Bassett, Juliette Lewis, Ralph Fiennes,

Charles Dutton, and Kathryn Bigelow. Additionally, she has received rave reviews for her theatre performances.

She is also a playwright and has written a successful play, which bridges the gap between Christians and Jews that broke records at its Los Angeles debut. She and her husband {{BB- care to include his name?} co-produced "Soaking in the Psalms," a prayer and meditation CD expected to be released in 2015.

Residing in, Florida, Dr. Bello is expanding her organization, **More Too Life**, where her advocacy, street outreach and mentoring programs for survivors are already underway.

Dr. Bello is married to a wonderful composer of gospel, jazz, and dance music. She and her husband hope to adopt children but are so happy to mentor many.

Aside from being extremely busy with ministering, mentoring, counseling, and many other duties, she is currently working on her second book.

Dr. Bello desires her readers always to remember to love your neighbor as yourself. Jesus didn't call those that persecuted Him evil or devils even when what they did was violent and not of God. Instead, He asked the Father to "forgive them for they know not what they do" (Luke 23:34, KJV).

Above all, Dr. Bello encourages others to go all the way and "Live Inside the Rainbow," to transform their lives beyond complacency to promise.

For information or to join the Fight to Stop Modern Day Slavery, visit our website at **www.moretoolife.org**.
Follow us on Twitter: @brookbello and @realmoretoolife
Follow us on Facebook.com/brook.bello
Email us for speaking engagements at **info@moretoolife.org**, or at **www.brookbello.com**.

Charles Dutton, and Kathryn Bigelow's Adaptation. She has received rave reviews for her theatre performances.

She is also a playwright and has written a successful play which bridges the gap between Christians and Jews that broke records at its Los Angeles debut. She and her husband [illegible] are [illegible] include [illegible] co-produced "Soaking in the Psalms" a [illegible] meditation [illegible] expected to be released in 2015.

Besides [illegible] is expanding her [illegible] New York [illegible] her advocacy [illegible] programs [illegible]

[illegible]

[illegible]

NOTES

Introduction1 "RJ Online —." *RJ Online* —. Centre for Justice and Reconciliation, 2009. Web. 1 Aug. 2013. <http://www.restorativejustice.org/>.
One of many websites that describe this new legal term of restorative justice
2 Ohio executes man who killed, raped 6-month-old, "USA TODAY: Latest World and US News." *USA Today*. Gannett, 1 May 2013. Web. **1**
<www.usatoday.com/story/news/nation/2013/05/...rape-baby/2126323/>.

3 DeFraia, Daniel. "World News | Breaking US News and International News Headlines - GlobalPost." *GlobalPost*. GlobalPost, 30 Apr. 2013. Web. 12 July 2013. < http://www.globalpost.com/dispatch/news/regions/asia-pacific/130430/4-year-old-girl-dies-india-after-horrific-rape.>.
4 Stossel, John. "Fox News." *Fox News*. FOX News Network, 1 Aug. 2013. Web. 12 Aug. 2013. http://www.foxnews.com/us/2013/08/01/ariel-castro-convicted-kidnapping-ohio-women-is-defiant-as-gets-life-plus-1000/#ixzz2akysRxWe>.

5 "The Neurobiology of Sexual Assault." Interview by John Laub. *National Institute of Justice*. National Institute of Justice, 3 Dec. 2012. Web. 25 July 2013. http://nij.gov/multimedia/presenter/presenter-campbell/data/resources/presenter-campbell-transcript.htm>.

Chapter 1

1 "Main Page." *Wikipedia*. Wikimedia Foundation, 08 Dec. 2013. Web. 12 Aug. 2013. "rainbow."
<https://en.wikipedia.org/wiki/Rainbow>.
2 "Strong's Greek: 5590. ψυχή (psuché) -- Breath, the Soul." *Strong's Greek: 5590. ψυχή (psuché) -- Breath, the Soul.* Online Parallel Bible Project, 2007. Web. 1 July 2013.
<http://biblesuite.com/greek/5590.htm>
3 "Vocabulary.com - English Dictionary." "cloud" *Vocabulary.com.* N.p., n.d. Web. 12 Aug. 2013.

*https://www.vocabulary.com/dictionary/*atmospheric%20phenomenon.

Chapter 2

1 ." *Merriam-Webster.* Merriam-Webster, n.d. Web. 15 Apr. 2013. < http://www.merriam-webster.com/dictionary/paraclete>.
"Strong's Greek: 3875. παράκλητος (paraklétos) -- Called to One's Aid." *Strong's Greek: 3875. παράκλητος (paraklétos) -- Called to One's Aid.* Online Parallel Bible Project, n.d. Web. 12 Aug. 2013. <http://biblesuite.com/greek/3875.htm>.
Greek Translation from one of my favorite sites on biblical words.

2 "Psychoanalysis." *Dictionary.com.* Dictionary.com, n.d. Web. 5 June 2013. <http://dictionary.reference.com/>.

Chapter 3

1 " Leaf, Caroline. "Dr. Leaf | Thought Life." *Dr. Leaf | Thought Life.* Dr. Caroline Leaf, n.d. Web. 1 Jan. 2012. <http://drleaf.com/thought_life.php>.
author and neuro-scientist who has studied the brain for 30 years.

2 Cherry, Kendra. "Brain Plasticity - Psychology Definition of the Week." *About.com Psychology.* N.p., 6 July 2012. Web. 12 Aug. 2013. <http://psychology.about.com/b/2012/07/06/brain-plasticity-psychology-definition-of-the-week.htm>.

3 "Kardia." *BibleStudyTools.com.* Salem Web Network, 1 Jan. 2008. Web. 12 Aug. 2013. <http://www.biblestudytools.com/lexicons/greek/kjv/kardia.html>. Popular Old and New Testament online word study

4 "Definition of Hippocampus in English." *Hippocampus: Definition Hippocampus in Oxford Dictionary.* Oxford University Press, n.d. Web. 10 Dec. 2012. http://oxforddictionaries.com/us/definition/american_english/hippocampus>.

5 Leaf, *of* Caroline. "Dr. Leaf | Thought Life." *Dr. Leaf | Thought Life.* Dr. Caroline Leaf, Phd, n.d. Web. 2 Jan. 2012. <http://drleaf.com/thought_life.php>.

6 "Statistics | RAINN | Rape, Abuse and Incest National Network." *Statistics | RAINN | Rape, Abuse and Incest National Network*. Rape Abuse & Incest National Network, n.d. Web. 5 Feb. 2013. <http://www.rainn.org/statistics>.
Nations largest anti-sexual violence organization and one of America's 100 best charities.

7 Helmenstine, Anne Marie, Ph.D. "How Much of Your Body Is Water?" *About.com Chemistry*. N.p., n.d. Web. 5 July 2013. <http://chemistry.about.com/od/waterchemistry/f/How-Much-Of-Your-Body-Is-Water.htm>.

8 "Rape Statistics." *Wikipedia*. Wikimedia Foundation, 08 Sept. 2012. Web. 12 Aug. 2013. <http://en.wikipedia.org/wiki/Rape_statistics>. "Rape Statistics." *Wikipedia*. Wikimedia Foundation, 08 Sept. 2012. Web. 12 Aug. 2013. <http://en.wikipedia.org/wiki/Rape_statistics>.
This average is found on several resources as well.

Chapter 4

1 "Speed of Sound." *Speed of Sound*. Wikipedia, n.d. Web. 1 June 2013. <http://www.princeton.edu/~achaney/tmve/wiki100k/docs/Speed_of_sound.html>.

2 "Speed of Light." *Wikipedia*. Wikimedia Foundation, n.d. Web. 10 July 2013. <http://en.wikipedia.org/wiki/Speed_of_light>.

3 Davidson, Kimberly. "Breaking the Cover Girl Mask." *Google Books*. Tate Publishing, 1 Dec. 2009. Web. 1 Aug. 2013. <http://books.google.com/books>.

4 "Pedophilia." *Wikipedia*. Wikimedia Foundation, 08 Feb. 2013. Web. 12 Aug. 2013. <http://en.wikipedia.org/wiki/Pedophilia>.

Chapter 7

1 "Koinonia." *Wikipedia*. Wikimedia Foundation, 25 July 2013. Web. 12 Aug. 2013. <http://en.wikipedia.org/wiki/Koinonia>.
"Strong's Greek: 2842. κοινωνία (koinónia) -- Fellowship." *Strong's Greek: 2842. κοινωνία (koinónia) -- Fellowship*. N.p., n.d. Web. 12 Aug. 2013. <http://biblesuite.com/greek/2842.htm>.

2 "Interview with Andrew Comiskey." Interview by Joseph Nicolosi, PhD. *Josephnicolosi.com.* Thomas Aquinas Psychological Clinic, n.d. Web. 1 June 2013.
<http://josephnicolosi.com/interview-with-andrew-comiskey/>.
Andrew Comiskey is an author who has written many books on sexual wholeness.

3 Ducharme, Stanley. "Web Design by Flyte New Mediaemail Web Master." *Pornography and Your Relationship.* Stanley Ducharme, Ph.D, n.d. Web. 12 June 2013.
<http://www.stanleyducharme.com/resources/pornography.html
>.
Dr. Ducharme does sex therapy and treats issues with relationships, addictions and sexual compulsions.

Chapter 8

1 "Arba'een." *Wikipedia.* Wikimedia Foundation, n.d. Web. 02 Aug. 2013. <http://en.wikipedia.org/wiki/Arba%27een>
I was there and saw it first hand with Muslim friends some who are now Christians and others who are still Muslim, but they took me nonetheless

2 Boe, John. "Actions Speak Lounder Than Words." *Non-verbal Communication: Actions Speak Louder Than Words.* Hodu.com, 2007. Web. 12 May 2013. <http://www.hodu.com/louder.shtml>.

Chapter 9

1 Kuhn, Thomas. "File: Duck-Rabbit Illusion.jpg." *Wikimedia.org.* Wikimedia Foundation, n.d. Web. 1 Mar. 2011.
<http://commons.wikimedia.org/wiki/File:Duck-Rabbit_illusion.jpg>.
Source: Jastrow, J. (1899). The mind's eye. Popular Science Monthly, 54, 299-312.
This media file is in the ***public domain*** *in the United States. This applies to U.S. works where the copyright has expired, often because its first publication occurred prior to January 1, 1923.*

2 Thomas Kuhn, *The Structure of Scientific Revolutions* (3rd edn., p. 114).

3 "The Neurobiology of Sexual Assault." Interview by John Laub. *National Institute of Justice*. National Institure of Justice, 3 Dec. 2012. Web. 25 July 2013. <http://nij.gov/>.

4 Chen, Allison. "Stockholm Syndrome." *Stockholm Syndrome.* Citelighter, n.d. Web. 1 July 2013. <http://www.citelighter.com/science/psychology/knowledgecards/stockholm-syndrome>.
Stockholm syndrome is n amed after the Norrmalmstorg robbery of Kreditbanken at Norrmalmstorg in Stockholm, Sweden, in which several bank employees were held hostage in a bank vault from August 23 to August 28, 1973.

5 "Ruby McCollum." *Rediff Pages.* Rediff On the Net, n.d. Web. 5 May 2013. <http://pages.rediff.com/ruby-mccollum/844599>.

6 Tanzi, Rudolph, K. and Chopra, Deepak. Super Brain. Harmony Crown, 2012.

7 Kuhn, Thomas. "File: Duck-Rabbit Illusion.jpg." *Wikimedia.org.* Wikimedia Foundation, n.d. Web. 1 Mar. 2011. <http://commons.wikimedia.org/wiki/File:Duck-Rabbit_illusion.jpg>.
Source: Jastrow, J. (1899). The mind's eye. Popular Science Monthly, 54, 299-312.
This media file is in the **public domain** *in the United States. This applies to U.S. works where the copyright has expired, often because its first publication occurred prior to January 1, 1923.*

8 "Helen Keller." *Wikipedia.* Wikimedia Foundation, n.d. Web. 13 June 2013. <http://en.wikipedia.org/wiki/Helen_Keller>.

9, 10 Mercy, James. Email interview. May 7, 2013

Chapter 11

1 Aslin, Richard N., Jenny R. Newport, and Elissa L. Newport. "Computation of Conditional Probability Statistics by 8-Month-Old Infants." *Computation of Conditional Probability Statistics by 8-Month-Old*

Infants. Psychological Science Journal, n.d. Web. 1 July 2013. <http://pss.sagepub.com/content/9/4/321.short>.

2 "Parakaleo." *BibleStudyTools.com.* N.p., n.d. Web. 1 Nov. 2012. <http://www.biblestudytools.com/lexicons/greek/nas/parakaleo.html>.

Chapter 12

1 Pounds, Keith. "The Importance of Fathers: Statistical Compilation by the South Carolina Fathers Initiative." *Keith Pounds Conservative and Libertarian Views.* N.p., 14 Jan. 2012. Web. 10 June 2013. <http://keithpounds.com/?p=1303>.

Chapter 14

1 "Industry." *Merriam-Webster Online Dictionary.* Merriam-Webster, n.d. Web. 03 July 2013. <http://www.merriam-webster.com/dictionary/industry>.

2 "Industry." *Merriam-Webster Online Dictionary.* Merriam Webster, n.d. Web. 03 July 2013.< <http://en.wikipedia.org/wiki/Safe_harbor_(law)>

To order SURVIVOR DVD or digital download, visit: http://www.cinecliq.com/movie/533

To arrange a screening of the film, visit: www.MoreTooLife.org.

www.ingramcontent.com/pod-product-compliance
Lightning Source LLC
Chambersburg PA
CBHW051945090426
42741CB00008B/1281

* 9 7 8 0 9 6 5 4 4 1 5 2 0 *